IT HAPPENED IN
IDAHO

It Happened In Series

IT HAPPENED IN
IDAHO

Randy Stapilus

TWODOT®

GUILFORD, CONNECTICUT
HELENA, MONTANA
AN IMPRINT OF THE GLOBE PEQUOT PRESS

A · TWODOT® · BOOK

The publisher gratefully acknowledges Ken Reid, Idaho State Archaeologist, and Larry R. Jones, Idaho State Historian, for reviewing this manuscript for historical accuracy.

Cover art © 2002 by Lisa Harvey, Helena, Montana

Library of Congress Cataloging-in-Publication Data is available.

ISBN 0-7627-1026-8

Manufactured in the United States of America
First Edition/First Printing

Contents

Preface

Idaho is such a divided state it defies easy description. The south is swathed by the flat, dry Snake River Plain; the west, east, and north are an amalgam of barren foothills, lush farmland, and tree-covered peaks. Idaho's middle is occupied by high and jagged mountains, severely limiting travel. Its only north-south road is commonly called "the goat trail" because of its ruggedness. The reasons for settlement as well as the economic and social bases in the north and south and east and west are radically different. The state even is said to have three capitals: Boise; Spokane, Washington; and Salt Lake City, Utah. It is split between two time zones—Mountain and Pacific—but the dividing line does not run north to south, as in some other states, but east to west.

The stories in this collection come from all over Idaho, and they reflect the diverse history and divided nature of the state—divisions that endure today.

Credit for a book about this divided state likewise has to be divided. Linda Watkins, Marty Peterson, Jim Weatherby, and the staffs of the Idaho State Library and Idaho State Historical Society were a great help in providing ideas and perspective on Idaho; and editor Charlene Patterson and artist Lisa Harvey shaped this book. Thanks to everyone who helped.

Shaping Stones

• 9000 B.C. •

The sun was setting, light was fading, and the hunters hurried to prepare their campfire for the night. There was urgency to their activity because the night was cool and getting colder.

The hunters were in a valley, but it was a high valley that could only be reached by climbing over mountains first. In the lowering light, the nomadic band could see high, jagged peaks off to the north and lower ones to the south. This valley was not an especially good place to stay. There was little water, just a few thin streams here and there, and few plants—mainly sagebrush and the camas plant, which provided some sustenance. The high desert was hot in the summer and cold in the winter. There was no real value in sticking around in this type of country.

But the hunters were here for a reason. Big game wandered through the area, following the streams down from the mountains, grazing on the valley's vegetation. Deer, bears, bison, and other animals came through on regular migrations. They had attracted the attention of this band of hunters, who in their explorations had found this valley crossroads. Here, the hunters also found small, hard stones—obsidian, mainly—that they could use. By day, in addition to hunting, they kept a lookout for stone quarries, though the best sites were several dozen miles away, south over the low mountains, or even farther over the hills to the west.

In the firelight the hunters prepared their weapons, pounding flakes from the core of the stones they had found and placing them under the campfire, heat-treating them. It took about eight hours to get the stones just right for reshaping. Once they were ready, the hunters turned the stones into sharp killing tools—points. The hunters used small rocks or sometimes part of an antler to hammer the stone into a sharp, V-shaped point. The points were almost always three to four inches long and less than an inch wide. After they shaped them, the hunters attached the points to sticks, or shafts, and used them to bring down game.

Sometimes the points were used as articles of trade when bands of hunters encountered each other. Some of the stone carvers were more skilled than others, and the best looking of the points—now called Clovis points, after the place in New Mexico where a large cache of them was first found—were highly prized. Sometimes the points were lost, or left behind, or came loose from their sticks, or remained buried under the campfire. And some of them were stored and simply never recovered.

About eleven thousand years later, as William Simon was using a bulldozer and carryall to move dirt on his farm near Fairfield, in the Camas Valley in central Idaho, he looked into the shallow trough he had made, which was about eighteen inches deep, and discovered several flinty little spear points. He called some neighbors to help him look around, and they found more.

He brought them to the attention of researchers at Idaho State University in Pocatello and at a state museum in Boise. The researchers were astounded at the find: These points were much older than any found before in Idaho. The researchers started a new wave of efforts to reconstruct the lives of Idaho's earliest residents who, it turned out, had lived in the area much earlier than previously suspected—as early as 9000 B.C.

Much about the day-to-day lives of Idaho's first residents remains a mystery, but the small items they left behind, such as the shaped stones, give us clues about these early people and their lives in what would become the "Gem State."

Lewis and Clark Meet the Nez Percé

· 1805 ·

Captain William Clark had no sense of any special danger when he and a few of the soldiers in his expedition walked out of the forest and into a clearing in a high meadow. Clark saw a few small animals but no people. He walked awhile, until he spotted three small Indian boys playing in the field.

Clark had seen few people besides the members of his expedition in recent days, and he wanted to make contact with these Indians. The expedition he led with Meriwether Lewis was in serious trouble, and it needed help.

The explorers approached, but the boys ran off, first hiding in the woods, then sprinting to their village. They were Ni Mii Pu, now called Nez Percé, and their message of strange-looking people—if people they were—sent an instant alarm through the camp. Some of the members of the tribe urged that the interlopers be killed immediately. The risks involved in letting them continue on, invading the tribal homeland, were too great.

They would not have had much difficulty dispatching the white men. On this day, September 22, 1805, on the Weippe plain in north central Idaho, the expedition had come as close as it ever would to a premature end.

The Lewis and Clark Expedition had left St. Louis, Missouri, in May 1804, and by the time they met these Native

Americans in what is now northern Idaho, they had been moving west for nearly a year and a half. It was a rigorous journey, far from help of any kind. They had spent their first winter in North Dakota—not an easy place to live during the winter months. Their encounters with Native Americans had been widely varied; some native people were friendly, some were not.

The expedition had just passed through one of the most difficult parts of its journey, crossing the Rocky Mountains, and the men were exhausted and concerned because another winter was fast approaching, and snow was already falling in the high elevations. They had eaten mainly wolf and crayfish and, occasionally, pheasant, when it was available. At times they were reduced to eating bear oil. Meriwether Lewis worried about the whole group becoming desperately ill before long; as he would become. Clark had been thrown from his horse and had injured his hip; he kept moving only with difficulty.

Clark wrote in his journal about this time, "Capt. Lewis verry sick . . . most of the Party Complaining. . . . I am a little unwell."

Lewis was so sick he had to stay in the main camp while Clark's scouting expedition went in search of food and human help. Clark's group might have walked into disaster. But Nez Percé legend says that an old woman named Wetxuwiis persuaded the other members of the village not to harm the explorers. She said that years before she had been captured and taken far east—so far that she saw a series of very large lakes—but a group of whites had helped her to escape and come home.

Chief Red Bear found Clark and escorted him and his men to the village lodge. There they were given food—salmon, and flour made from the camas plant, which didn't agree with the travelers. Clark appreciated the gifts, however, and reciprocated with a medallion from President Thomas Jefferson, who had commissioned the expedition. The exchange of gifts helped improve everyone's attitude. Clark then bought a load of salmon and other supplies and sent it back to Lewis.

Lewis and Clark shook hands with the tribal leaders, a practice the Nez Percé found peculiar but evidently friendly. The travelers had no clue that they had been in great danger. None of their travel journals reflect anything other than a friendly reception by the Nez Percé.

Before long, Nez Percé from villages around the region came to the Weippe plain to see the travelers. They showed the expedition members how to build a canoe more efficiently: Burn logs with pitch and dry grass, they were told, and then chop them into shape with an obsidian ax. This wound up improving the efficiency of the often-waterlogged expedition.

A chief named Twisted Hair drafted a map showing them the path they could take from the Clearwater River downhill to the Snake River then on to the Columbia River, which flowed into the Pacific Ocean. Clark double-checked the map as he traveled along and found it accurate, and the expedition mostly followed the route it laid out.

So friendly was the new relationship that one Nez Percé traveled by land along the Clearwater River ahead of the floating explorers, telling other tribes about the travelers and asking them to give them safe passage. All of them did.

The explorers reached the Pacific in late November and spent an unpleasant but safe winter at Fort Clatsop in what is now Oregon. The following spring, they returned through Idaho the way they had come, again meeting up with the Nez Percé, who again provided food and guides.

There is a possibility that Idaho had visitors of European descent before the members of the Lewis and Clark Expedition, but if there were, their presence is lost to history. Lewis and Clark have given us the earliest written record of what is now Idaho, and their travels through the state have been recorded in signpost and celebration.

Rendezvous at Pierre's Hole

· 1832 ·

Over on one side of the encampment, early on the hot morning of July 8, 1832, John Jacob Astor's American Fur Company had set up shop. Three miles north, across Teton Creek but straight up a path in the middle of the broad valley, the Rocky Mountain Fur Company was open for business. Nearby, several smaller companies, such as the Bea-Sinclair, and some large ones with limited presence in the area, such as the Hudson's Bay Company, also were represented. Hundreds of people had traveled by foot or by horse or mule, through an area where few trails existed, from a radius of hundreds of miles. Many had to come over or find their way around the jagged Teton Mountains. There was no town here. This was more like a trade convention, and the companies—and the trappers from whom they bought and sold—were in tough and often bitter competition.

This encampment—this rendezvous, as the French-speaking trappers preferred to call it—was temporary and would be gone ten days hence. But these were ten days the participants would never forget.

The place was Pierre's Hole, a valley named for a Canadian trapper who had died nearby, now the Teton Valley of Idaho, on the west side of the Teton Range, which towers above. It is just across the mountains from present-day Jackson, Wyoming.

The legends of the trapping world were here: Jim Bridger, Joe Meek, Bill Sublette, Alexander Sinclair, Jean Baptiste Gervais, among them. They were joined by bands of Nez Percé and Flathead Indians who were there to trade in pelts as well.

Many of these trappers rarely saw another human being for most of the year and had few opportunities other than this to sell their wares and pick up needed supplies. Because the men rarely visited towns and trading camps were hundreds of miles away, the rendezvous was their main chance to buy or swap for such things as horses, food supplies, guns and ammunition, liquor, and clothes and tobacco, medicines, and shoes.

They could obtain all this and more because in the first part of the nineteenth century, pelts were enormously valuable. They had been a rage in Europe among the fashionable for more than two hundred years, among the less fashionable for half as long, and in American cities for several decades. At the same time, furbearing animals were being wiped out of most of the heavily populated areas of Europe and America; western North America was at this time one of the great remaining untapped reserves of beaver, fox, mink, otter, and other animal pelts.

Crammed into a ten-day period, the rendezvous was also their entertainment for the year. That fact tended to ensure that rendezvous were lively events. Most of them were held in what is now Wyoming and Utah; just two were held in Idaho, both at Pierre's Hole. They had started in 1825, just as the fur trade was building; by the end of the 1830s, the trade had diminished again and would soon fade. By many accounts the 1832 rendezvous, at the very peak of the fur trade and competition, was the liveliest of them all.

The rendezvous started with the arrival of William Sublette, a key middleman with the Rocky Mountain Fur Company and bringer of most of the supplies.

Joe Meek, writing in his journal, described what happened next:

When Captain Sublette's goods were opened and distributed among the trappers and Indians, then began the usual gay carousal; and the "fast young men" of the mountains outvied each other in all manner of mad pranks. In the beginning of their spree many feats of horsemanship and personal strength were exhibited, which were regarded with admiring wonder by the sober and inexperienced New Englanders under Mr. [Nathaniel] Wyeth's command. And as nothing stimulated the vanity of the mountain men like an audience of this sort, the feats they performed were apt to astonish themselves.

But the horse-racing, fine riding, wrestling and all the manlier sports, soon degenerated into the baser exhibitions of a "crazy drunk" condition. The vessel in which the trapper received and carried about this supply of alcohol was one of the small camp kettles. "Passing around" this clumsy goblet very freely, it was not long before a goodly number were in the condition just named, and ready for any mad freak whatever. It is reported by several of the mountain men that on the occasion of one of the "frolics," one of their number seized a kettle of alcohol, and poured it over the head of a tall, lank, redheaded fellow, repeating as he did so the baptismal ceremony. No sooner had he concluded than another man with a lighted stick touched him with the blaze, when in an instant he was enveloped in flames. Luckily some of the company had sense enough to perceive his danger, and began beating him with pack-saddles to put out the blaze.

There were boasts and fights, exhibitions of strength and ability to withstand pain, and competitions with guns and bows.

As the event began to break up, two things happened. One was a battle, only a few miles from the camp, with Blackfeet tribesmen; the trappers and their allies prevailed, but the area was then deemed hazardous. The other event was an agreement between the two largest competing companies, American Fur and Rocky Mountain Fur, over territories and prices. It led to organization in the fur business and establishment of more stable trade routes and trading centers, which led to the decline of the rendezvous.

Today several places in Idaho—the largest is at American Falls—have revived the rendezvous with demonstrations of mountain man activities. But the original mountain men were long gone from Idaho, and the rendezvous a romantic memory, by the time the first emigrants from the eastern states started to settle there.

Henry Spalding's Bible
· 1839 ·

The balding, thick-bearded, fierce-eyed preacher was ambitious and determined, and he was about to become the first man in present-day Idaho to use a printing press—to begin, if not to finish, printing a Bible. But then, Henry Spalding began much more than he finished.

There may have been some one-upmanship in his efforts because of the reasons that had brought him to this remote place on a branch of the Clearwater River. Henry Spalding and his wife, Eliza, had arrived a couple years before, after a long journey from the east, at Walla Walla in eastern Washington. They and another missionary couple, Marcus and Narcissa Whitman, had arrived to found a mission in that area, and the four hard workers made progress for a time. But some years before, Henry Spalding and Narcissa Whitman had been romantically involved, and that sparked a series of quarrels between them. The arguments became louder and louder, and the couples eventually agreed they could not stay together. Finally, the Spaldings agreed to move out and set up a new mission farther inland, in what is now northern Idaho, near a number of Nez Percé tribal settlements.

A vigorous man, Spalding built one piece of the new settlement after another—by himself in some cases and with help from his wife and Indians in others. To begin, he built a mission house, eventually upgraded it to a two-story building with fire-places on each side, where he held church services.

He built a sawmill and a gristmill. He built a school, and Eliza became its teacher. He planted an orchard. He started the first irrigated farm in the area and persuaded some of the Nez Percé to join in the farming effort and in 1837 even to skip their annual buffalo hunt, a highlight of the year's activities. And, of course, he preached the gospel as regularly as he could.

All that was still not enough. In 1839 he bought and arranged to have shipped all the way from Hawaii to his set-tlement of Lapwai, the first printing press ever seen in Idaho or even in the Pacific Northwest. It came across the Pacific Ocean by ship, over the Cascade Mountains and deserts by wagon, and finally, the last stretch from the Walla Walla area on a river-boat personally captained by Spalding himself.

His plan was to use it to print papers and even books to be used at the school and in the education of the Indians. His first effort on the press was an eight-page reader for children. Soon after, he tried more ambitious projects, such as a printing of the New Testament's Gospel of John.

All this might have been enough to satisfy many people, or at least keep them occupied. Not Henry Spalding. He still ar-gued with everyone in sight—with, as one person wrote, "many of the Indians and all of the non-Indians." His ferocious, cantankerous style limited his effectiveness among the Nez Percé, and tribal members gradually stayed away from him. So did the missionaries sent to help him; there was a steady turnover. He even wrote about himself in his diary: "Had some humiliating thoughts of myself last night. Looked upon myself the most ungrateful, useless sinful one in the Mission. Thought if I could see my brothers and sisters once more I would cast myself at their feet and beg pardon for many offenses."

In 1847 Henry Spalding, concerned about the safety of his family, left Lapwai after Marcus and Narcissa Whitman and oth-ers at their mission were killed by renegade members of the

Cayuse tribe. The minister remained restless, moving to Oregon and twice back to the Clearwater River country, where he died in 1874. His remarkable early mission did not last; it closed when he left.

But the Nez Percé remembered what Spalding had taught them. The tribe's headquarters is today located at Lapwai, near the original Spalding settlement. And just a few miles north of there, on the banks of the Clearwater, is the small community of Spalding and a state historical park commemorating one of Idaho's earliest ministers, farmers—and printers.

Building the Cataldo Mission

· 1842 ·

Father Pierre De Smet, Catholic priest and missionary in the wild western lands, stood with a group of Coeur d'Alene Indians to whom he was teaching the precepts of Catholicism. Working with a local interpreter, he already had translated into their language several key passages: the Ten Commandments, the Lord's Prayer, the Hail Mary.

Now, on this spring morning, with a translator again nearby, he taught them these passages one by one, asking each person to remember one verse—and eventually learn them all from each other. Knowing he could not stay long, De Smet wanted to build something that would last after he had moved on. He did.

He was pleased at his progress in the short time he'd been there. Within a few days, the group knew all of the passages by heart. De Smet somehow connected with the Coeur d'Alenes, establishing a bond.

Father De Smet had come through the area as a sidetrip. He had first visited the Flathead Indians to the east, and in this spring of 1842, he was headed west again, toward the Colville area. But he stopped to meet with the Coeur d'Alenes, and he set off a series of events that would change their lives forever.

He stayed only a short time, but he promised to send back another priest who would establish a permanent mission building. He did just that a couple of years later, sending Father Nicholas Point from a mission a couple of hundred miles to the east to set up the new building.

It took awhile, and there were a few false starts. The first site they considered turned out to be flooded occasionally by the St. Joe River, so they searched for a new location on higher ground. Then, Father Anthony Ravelli arrived to take over, and he pushed the project through to completion. He drew detailed plans for a main building and nine smaller ones and brought all the tools needed, from augurs to axes to ropes. One of the volunteers, John Ruskin, declared, "When we build, let us think that we build forever."

The work was not easy, however. It took Ravelli, several other church workers, and many members of the tribe almost a decade to complete. Ravelli had designed the building in a style called Greek Revival; on its completion, the large, impressive building measured 90 feet by 40 feet. Timbers were fitted inside each other through drilled holes. The walls were covered with straw and river mud.

The Coeur d'Alenes were impressed by the big building and the work that went into it, and they stopped their traveling ways and stayed to farm in the area around the new mission. They remained, and many still remain, active in the church as a result of that early missionary work. Though the Coeur d'Alene tribe now is based on a reservation some miles from the mission, many tribal members still feel a close association with it.

Mission operations were taken over in 1865 by Father Joseph Cataldo. His work with the tribe and other newcomers to the territory was so extensive that the area, and eventually the mission, was named for him. Over the years, as the panhandle of Idaho developed, the mission became a regular stop for travelers.

The old mission has been refurbished several times, most extensively in the 1920s and in the 1970s. Visible from Interstate 90 east of Coeur d'Alene, it stands today in seemingly pristine condition, the oldest building still standing in Idaho.

Father De Smet built the foundation only with spirit. But like his successor Father Ravelli, he built it to last.

Treacherous Three-Island Crossing

· 1845 ·

On the night before Samuel Hancock's wagon train approached Three-Island Crossing, its leaders decided that caution was in order. They camped a couple of miles southwest of the crossing and sent two men to scout it—to see how deep it was, how fast the river current ran, and how much trouble the wagon train would have fording it.

The crossing on the Snake River looked deceptively peaceful. The river was bent at a sharp angle and spread out at this point, split by three small islands (two of which were used for crossing), and seemed calm. Those who tried to cross it soon learned otherwise. Someone saw the two scouts walk into the river. After that, they were seen no more that night.

People in the camp awaited their return throughout the night. The next morning, four men went in search of them. Hours later, they found signs of blood and bits of clothing. Off the shoreline a mile away, they found the body of one of the men. They buried it then kept looking for the other man. As night started to fall, they gave up the search. The other scout was never found.

The Hancock party had just reached one of the most dangerous parts of the Oregon Trail.

The year was 1845, and they had started on the trail at St. Joseph, Missouri, along with so many others. It was the second year of large-scale emigrant traffic on the Oregon Trail, increasing each year until peaking in 1852, when ten thousand emigrants headed west. They brought wagons, oxen, horses, and food. But by the time they reached the great Snake River rapids in the deserts of southern Idaho, the food was nearly gone. They summoned enough energy to trade with Indians for the salmon the natives speared at rapids that ran through the Hagerman Valley, but after that—after long, dusty travel under the searing August sun—they were in no condition to face extreme challenges.

That is when they hit the worst of them—one of the most feared spots on the whole Oregon Trail: the crossing at Three-Island.

Hancock and his people knew they didn't absolutely have to cross from the south side of the Snake River to the north at this spot. But they knew the road on the south side would soon get much worse, and there was no way to avoid a major river crossing somewhere up ahead. Three-Island was bad, but it was the best spot available. Once across, the road was mostly level and well broken for many miles to come, and some military protection at Fort Boise lay ahead.

Others had faced the same choices. Less than two years before, John Fremont, known as "the Pathfinder," had written in his journal:

> About two o'clock we had arrived at the ford where the road crosses to the right bank of the Snake River. An Indian was hired to conduct us through the ford, which proved impracticable for us, the water sweeping way the howitzer and nearly drowning the mules, which we were obliged to extricate by cutting them out of the harness. The river is expanded into a little bay, in which there are two islands, across which is the road of the ford; and the emigrants had passed by placing two of their heavy wagons abreast

of each other, so as to oppose a considerable mass against the body of water.

As Hancock surveyed the crossing, he found a river about 200 yards wide, "which was very rapid and deep."

Hancock and his party planned carefully, accounting for the fast and heavy stream. They propped up the beds of the wagons. Teams of men on horseback—horses and men chained together so none would be swept away—carried them across.

In this way, Hancock later wrote, "We reached the opposite bank safely, though some of the smaller cattle were forced to swim."

The Hancock party eventually reached safety in Oregon.

Several years later, in 1869, a ferry service across that portion of the Snake River was founded a couple of miles upstream from Three-Island, and what is now the city of Glenns Ferry grew up around it. Three-Island Crossing became a state park in 1971, and every summer a group of "pioneers" demonstrates how Oregon Trail travelers crossed the river.

Franklin Founded
· 1860 ·

The Mormon farmers walking north across the Cache Valley thought they were doing something incremental—helping to grow their church and expand its reach—but not anything especially remarkable on that cool day in early April 1860. They were leaving the town of Logan behind and taking their families, wagons, and supplies just a couple of days' walk north, across the flat, high valley where snow was slowly easing back and moving up the steep mountainsides.

They thought of themselves as pioneers in only a small way. They had been asked by Brigham Young, president of the Church of Jesus Christ of Latter-day Saints, to expand the reach of the church's Utah settlement by just a little bit. They would be staying in the same valley as Logan, where services were available.

When they got to a small river, the Cub River, they stopped and decided to found the new town there. From this spot they could see directly down the valley toward Logan. They discussed a name for the town and decided to name it Franklin, for Franklin Richards, an apostle in the church.

Then they started marking out land the way other Utah pioneers had done it. First they drew a quadrangle about 500 yards by 330 yards. They stripped down their wagons so that only the undercarriages were left and used them to carry logs to the quad. Then they built cabins for the new settlers in a fort style with all the doors facing inside, toward the quad.

They worked hard that spring because they knew they would need crops that year. They dug an irrigation ditch to pull water from what was called Spring's Creek, and the settlers planted both small vegetable gardens and large fields of other crops, including oats and barley, that could be sold. They built a small schoolhouse. By the end of summer, they were able to trade for supplies and send traders 100 miles south to Salt Lake City to obtain more.

Their sense of having accomplished their mission was complete soon after that when Brigham Young and a group of other church officials arrived to tour the new town, to praise the work that had been done, and to appoint a bishop.

Over the next few years, the settlement was expanded. Because trees were available only a few miles away, church officials decided it might be beneficial to have a sawmill. Brigham Young personally arranged to buy one; it was shipped from east of the Mississippi up the Missouri River to Montana. From there it was hauled overland. Franklin kept growing, and the Utah legislature incorporated it as a village in 1868.

Not until four years later did anyone realize that the farmers of Franklin had done something much more remarkable than simply found another small Utah farm town. A survey was run, and Franklin turned out to have been founded just across the border in Washington Territory, which in 1863 became Idaho Territory. The farmers had inadvertently founded Idaho's first permanent town.

Franklin never became one of Idaho's largest communities, but it has more than just survived—it has prospered. It grew significantly in the 1870s when a rail line was run north from Logan. And in recent years, when so many farm communities in Idaho have struggled, Franklin has fared well specifically because of its border location. Many Utah residents cross the border here for reasons far different than those of Franklin's founders—they buy lottery tickets and imported beers that are unavailable back home.

The Planned Boomtown

· 1861 ·

Elias Davidson Pierce, who favored the strictly honorary title "Captain," engaged in a long series of reckless, haphazard, spur-of-the-moment, and failed projects in his colorful life. That made his involvement with Idaho an unusual, even uncharacteristic, thing. The creation of Idaho's first mining boomtown, and the opening of the area as a mining region, was anything but impulsive. It was carefully thought out. It had to be if Pierce was going to overcome the many obstacles in his way. He must have understood the difficulties because he'd overcome so many already.

A native of Indiana, Pierce first came west to serve in the Mexican-American War, which may have incited his wanderlust and possibly his gambling spirit, as well. After the war, he became engaged to Rebecca Jones, but he soon left her behind to travel west again, first to try to make a fortune in the California mines (he didn't) and then in the Pacific Northwest fur trade (where he did better).

On an expedition inland he spotted country on the Clearwater River that he thought had potential as a goldfield; it was geographically similar to places he'd seen in California. But that region was soon declared to be part of—or, because accounts differ, was only accessible through—the Nez Percé Indian

Reservation, and both tribal members and federal officials said mining expeditions were strictly banned from that area.

Pierce never stopped thinking about the area, though. Even while in California, where he became the first man to climb Mount Shasta, and while serving in the California legislature, he thought about what he was sure were goldfields in the Clearwater River area. He even moved to Walla Walla and worked as a farmer for four years to be closer to the area, though he was blocked from returning by federal officials and tribal leaders. In the fall of 1860, promising to avoid the reservation boundary but taking along an Indian guide who would steer him through the trouble spots, he took a dozen men on a secret expedition to the Weippe plains high above the Clearwater. There he found what he was sure were indications of gold.

That winter, back in Walla Walla, he led a group of several dozen conspirators determined to rush for gold in this new country. Knowing they would face opposition as they tried to work their claim, and realizing they would have one chance to make good, they planned their effort down to small details. They rebuilt a string of eight houses in Walla Walla, merged them, and in this makeshift factory created a boomtown, building sluice boxes for the mines, writing mining laws, even laying out a new city—Pierce City.

In the spring they floated inland, up the Clearwater, and started to work—and in fact, they found gold. Word shot through the West. Miners from British Columbia to Southern California poured in, and neither the tribe nor the federal agents could stop the flow. The attention of federal officials was in any event distracted at that particular moment because the rush to Pierce occurred just as the Civil War erupted.

The towns that appeared in that area—Oro Fino and Pierce—were true mining boomtowns. Thousands of people arrived in 1861, and dozens of businesses sprang up out of thin air. Pierce became Idaho's first county seat, and its first public building, a courthouse, was built here. So fast did people arrive that this became the most populous district in Washington Territory for a short time, and the territorial legislature even authorized building a road from Lewiston to the Pierce area. Concerns about incursions into the Nez Percé reservation were forgotten (except, of course, by the Nez Percé).

The gold deposits may have been visible, but they were also shallow. No more than $3.6 million in gold ever has been extracted from the area. In little over a year, most of the miners were gone, rushed off to new Idaho boomtowns to the south, at Florence, Warrens, and Idaho City.

Pierce, mostly depopulated, straggled on for several more decades until the new century brought a new realization—the thick stands of trees in the area were valuable. Timber companies set up shop, and Pierce and nearby communities became timber towns. They remained so for a full century; only recently have most of the mills in the area closed. The future of Pierce is unclear. As it enters a new century, Pierce is also entering another era.

As for the town's namesake, Elias Pierce lost most of his gold money in a series of failed businesses. Then he heard another man was courting his Indiana fiancée, Rebecca Jones, whom he had not seen in twenty years. He raced back to Indiana and persuaded her to marry him. The two of them settled down in Indiana, living on his veteran's pension, until he died in 1897.

The Bear River Battle

· 1863 ·

The weather was cold and gloomy when the march started; the early January morning sky was darkly overcast, the ground covered with snow. The foot soldiers headed out from the tiny settlement of Franklin and marched northwest across the new farm fields to Bear River. Their progress was slowed by the frequent mud.

Colonel Patrick Connor, in overall command, positioned his faster-moving cavalry on the flat plain with a small canyon carved into it by the Bear River. In the canyon was an Indian encampment, a band of Shoshones, alerted to the arrival of the troops and carefully watching their movements. Both sides seemed to know this was the climax of years of conflict and that a great deal would be settled in the next few hours.

For years this band of Shoshones had been antagonizing westward-bound settlers in the Wasatch Mountains and the Big Hole country of Montana. They raided travelers on the Oregon Trail and other routes. Even other Indians, including more settled Shoshones, were wary of them. For their part the band was fighting against the destruction of their old hunting grounds as more and more newcomers arrived in their territory.

The conflict escalated. On both sides prisoners were taken and sometimes executed.

Then Patrick Connor arrived from California determined to suppress the Shoshones. Connor was a frustrated soldier, so eager to enter the battles of the Civil War that he offered to pay his own way east. His army superiors instead ordered him to monitor the settlements in Utah and to take action against the local Indians as he saw fit. Though unhappy about his placement in Utah, he was pleased to be allowed to fight the Indians.

As he rode on that January morning to within earshot of the Shoshone encampment, Connor heard a taunt from the canyon: "Come and get it! We're ready for you!" Deciding not even to wait until his infantry, still mired in mud, had arrived, Connor ordered his cavalry to attack.

At first, the Shoshones had the best of it. They had a protected position from which to fire, and Connor's cavalry made good targets. But once Connor had assessed the situation and his infantry had arrived, he realized something else: The Shoshones were trapped in the canyon.

He ordered separate groups of soldiers to enter the canyon on either side of the Shoshones, attacking them from each flank, while his main force kept them from climbing out of the canyon onto the plain. The few who did try to escape were mowed down. In the canyon the soldiers shot anyone who moved, women and children included.

More than thirty of the soldiers died, but the estimate of Indian deaths was at least three hundred. William Hull, a Mormon sent the next day from nearby Franklin to search for Indian survivors, wrote: "Never will I forget the scene, dead bodies were everywhere. I counted eight deep in one place and in several places they were three to five deep; all in all we counted nearly 400; two-thirds of this number being women and children." Connor, after filing his report on the battle, was promoted to brigadier general.

A few months later, five shaken Shoshone bands signed peace treaties with the United States. The band that participated in the battle at Bear River kept a low profile for several years and in 1868 signed the treaty that placed them on the Fort Hall reservation in eastern Idaho.

The Bear River battlefield, the bloodiest spot in Idaho history, is today located at the end of an obscure gravel road about 4 miles from the city of Preston, adjacent to Highway 91.

The Midnight Theft
of the Capital
· 1865 ·

The streets of Lewiston were mostly clear of people on this cold night in March, and that was part of the plan. Few people in town would notice the U.S. Army troops advancing on the city from the east.

The soldiers rode straight into the middle of town, past the newspaper office, the meeting center for the vigilantes, and the stores—the few still remaining after the recent boom years had faded.

They fired no weapons, for they were not going to war, though the town was almost set to explode with tension. There might have been violence, except that the soldiers had the benefit of surprise. They broke into the territorial jail, but they were not planning to release, or imprison, anyone.

They were after papers—official papers, including the official seal of the Idaho Territory. The papers had been placed in the jail and were tightly guarded by Lewistonians specifically to prevent territorial officials from taking them to Boise, which was exactly what the soldiers were here to do. The soldiers, under the direction of Territorial Secretary Clinton DeWitt Smith, swiftly broke in, overpowered the Lewiston residents, swept up the papers, and left town, headed south.

The location of the territorial capital had been bitterly disputed for the past two years. At the moment the Idaho Territory was created, on March 4, 1863, almost all of the population was centered in the mining camps not far from Lewiston. But by the time the territorial legislature met at the end of the year, those camps were closing and the new boomtowns were in what is now southern Idaho, not far from the small Oregon Trail supply town of Boise. When the legislature met in its second session in 1864, a majority of delegates were from the south, and they voted to move the capital to Boise.

There was even more to it. Idaho Territory then included most of what is now western Montana. To get to Lewiston delegates from Virginia City and other Montana mining camps had to travel by way of Salt Lake City, Reno, San Francisco, and Portland on a long, onerous trip.

Lewistonians by that time already were watching their town slide into depression. From a town of several thousand people, with more than three dozen businesses (and many hundreds of tents, resulting in the nickname "Ragtown"), it had declined rapidly to a village no more than a quarter as large. Those residents remaining were desperate to have Lewiston remain the capital because of the federal money that came with the designation. Fortunately for them, Idaho Territory did already have lawyers. They found that the territorial recordkeepers had done sloppy work, and some important records—including some legislative records—were missing. With the missing records as a pretext, Lewiston forces filed a lawsuit aimed at keeping the capital in place. The district judge who would hear the case was from Lewiston and likely to side with them.

The dispute grew so hot that the territorial governor vanished. Caleb Lyon, a politically connected New York socialite who had been given the governorship as a political favor, "turned to jelly," as one historian put it. He was kept under close observation by people in Lewiston until one day in fall 1864, he told people that he was going on a duck hunting trip and instead hot-footed it out of the territory, headed first to Walla Walla, Washington, then to Washington, D.C. He would not return to Idaho for most of a year, and then only to Boise, not Lewiston. (He was lured back by word of a get-rich-quick gold scheme that didn't pan out, and he didn't remain governor for long after that.) Idaho had no territorial government at all for several months.

As soon as they learned of Lyon's departure, a mob of Lewistonians seized the records and territorial seal at the capitol and dumped them in the local jail, where they were kept under round-the-clock watch. They also warned the few territorial employees left in town not to move them.

Their actions had to be taken seriously. Lewiston was a dangerous and violent place, virtually beyond the law. Shootouts on the streets were not unusual. There were few law officers, and fewer courts. Politics helped ratchet emotions even higher, because most of the residents of the new territory were Democrats who sympathized with the South in the Civil War, while the territorial officials were all Republicans appointed by Abraham Lincoln.

In early March 1865, Clinton DeWitt Smith, a new territorial secretary—in effect a lieutenant governor—arrived. Smith was despised by the Lewiston residents, who wrote him off as a simple-minded alcoholic (and he did die of alcoholism several months later). But Smith understood that the capital clearly had to move closer to the bulk of the population. He also had the determination Lyon lacked. Only days after arriving in Lewiston, Smith rode out to the army station at Fort Lapwai on the Nez Percé reservation, about a dozen miles away. He told the fort's commander that, as acting governor, he had civilian authority over the troops there. Under cover of night, Smith and a group of soldiers rode back to Lewiston, broke into the jail, grabbed the official territorial papers, and headed south. They were in effect taking the capital with them.

They arrived in Boise on April 14, to cheering crowds and a cannon salute. A downtown building was designated as a temporary capitol and the records were deposited there.

The court dispute continued for a time. The Lewiston judge did rule, as expected, that the capital should stay at Lewiston, but the territorial Supreme Court overruled him.

The "theft of the capital" never has been forgotten in Lewiston. Thomas Donaldson, a territorial official in the early 1870s, recalled that Lewiston "was practically wiped out of existence when she lost her proud possession, the seat of the territorial government." That anger resulted in ongoing efforts to split northern Idaho away from the south to join Washington State instead. Even today, a sign greets highway travelers arriving in town via the bridge across the Snake River from Pullman, Washington, noting proudly that Lewiston was Idaho's first capital.

From Slave to Legend
· 1872 ·

Charlie Bemis, a slight man with a low-key but engaging manner, was talking with a friend one day in 1890 in the doorway of his gambling house in the rugged mining town of Warren, when the grizzled miner and gunman named Johnny Cox walked in and threatened him.

Cox had made the mistake of playing poker with Bemis, a skillful card player, a few days earlier. This day, he leaned against a post and told Bemis, "When I get this cigarette rolled if you don't give me back that $150 you beat out of me at poker, I'm going to shoot your eye out."

Bemis was accustomed to threats and took no heed of this one. Unshaken, he calmly continued his conversation. This time he was wrong. Cox coolly rolled his cigarette, lit it, put it in his mouth, then took out his gun and fired at Bemis. He just missed Bemis's right eye, but the bullet went into his skull and lodged toward the back of his brain. Cox turned around and rode out of town.

Bemis's friends gathered around him. They lifted him off the floor, carried him home, and summoned a doctor from Grangeville, a ride of more than a day each way. When the physician finally arrived, he concluded, "Nothing can be done. He is too far gone."

He surely would have been a goner without the help of Polly, a Chinese woman who, according to local legend, he had won at another poker game almost eighteen years earlier.

Polly, as she was called in Warren, had lived in northern China until her father sold her to bandits for a season's worth of grain. She was sold several times more, eventually crossing the Pacific to San Francisco and traveling from there to Portland. In Portland she was sold for $2,500 to Hong King, who soon after left for Warren with Polly as his cook and slave.

Hong King also made the mistake of engaging in a poker game with Bemis, who had come into the country as a miner but preferred gambling. After winning almost everything else Hong King had, legend says he won Polly—and after that Hong King folded his hand and the next day left Warren.

Bemis put Polly to work as a cook and manager of a local boarding house that catered to miners and other visitors to the backcountry. Their relationship grew gradually closer, then on the day Bemis was shot, Polly took charge.

Turning physician, she performed surgery, removing the bullet with the help of a razor and cleaning and sealing the wound with her crochet hook. She treated him with herbs and folk remedies. A month later, Bemis was still alive and able to sit up in bed. He gradually returned to almost full activity over the next year.

Johnny Cox was eventually caught in Pocatello and convicted of assault with a deadly weapon. He served two years in prison and thereafter disappeared from sight.

But Polly's story was just beginning. She and Charlie Bemis were married in 1894, and they spent many years in Warren. Charlie Bemis's health continued to be precarious, so they finally left Warren and its gambling halls behind and homesteaded on the Salmon River, about 40 miles east of Riggins. First known as the Bemis Ranch, it has become known in the decades since as the "Polly Bemis Place."

There she became a fixture in the Idaho backcountry. She was in effect a nurse to anyone who needed medical attention; she was widely described as "The Angel of the Salmon River." The ranch was a regular stop for people in the area. It had the only garden in the region, and travelers regularly stocked up with fruits and vegetables.

In 1922 the Bemis house burned, and Charlie Bemis died two months later. Polly Bemis moved across the river where two friends, Charlie Shepp and Peter Klinkhammer, had set up another ranch. There she lived, an icon on the Salmon River, until her death in November 1933.

The Polly Bemis story has been recounted in books, articles, and even a movie called *A Thousand Pieces of Gold*. Many people every year experience it in a more direct way.

The Shepp Ranch is still alive, now as a vacation ranch for visitors, still accessible only by river travel. Tourists can visit the grave of Polly Bemis, moved in recent years from Grangeville back to the home she loved. And they can learn her unusual story first hand.

Conflict at White Bird Canyon

· 1877 ·

It was called a war. It was, more accurately, a flight, and on the morning of June 17, 1877, the Nez Percé were trapped.

This band was a part of the Nez Percé tribe led by Hin-mah-too-yah-lat-keht—called Chief Joseph by many non-Indians. They were in a position none of them had sought, and now they could only hope to battle their way out.

It was a hopeless place. In the White Bird Canyon, there was nowhere to go but up. To the north steep foothills waved all around, many of them much too steep to allow for a horse to climb; the Camas prairie lay on the other side. To the south lay the narrow Salmon River canyon, a death trap.

Their moves had become ever more constricted with time. Only a few decades before, as Joseph could remember from his younger days, they had roamed freely in the country around the Wallowa Mountains in what is now northeastern Oregon, occasionally ranging into Clearwater River country in Idaho.

Then came a series of treaties that limited the Nez Percé to ever-smaller areas in northern Idaho. But, as Joseph pointed out to federal officials, neither he nor any of the leaders of his band had made any such agreements.

At one point President Ulysses S. Grant gave Joseph and his people what they wanted—a reservation in the Wallowa Mountains country. But white settlers protested and Grant changed his mind, ordering Joseph to the Idaho reservation within thirty days, a very short period of time to prepare for and make such a trip. Joseph reluctantly agreed and was leading his band through Idaho territory when three young men from his group broke off and killed four settlers in retaliation for past wrongs. That was enough to set the band and the U.S. Army at war.

But it was a one-sided war. Joseph's band wanted only to escape and didn't want to fight at all. Their plan was to travel into the Rocky Mountains and eventually north to Canada, where they could live in peace. But mid-June found them in the White Bird Canyon, with high mountains all around, and army troops under Captain David Perry nearby.

They held off firing until the army troops, clad in blue uniforms, were close in view. The Nez Percé sent messengers to the army commanders, hoping to find a peaceful way out. But when soldiers fired at them—and missed—hopes for a peaceful solution ended.

The battle that followed has been described as a strategic masterwork on the part of the Nez Percé. Recent studies show that this is myth. The Nez Percé fought as individuals, not as part of a close-knit unit; there was no chain of command. Joseph was there and participated in the battle, but probably simply as another warrior. The Nez Percé were every bit as skillful as their reputation, however. Outnumbered and outgunned, they fought that day guerrilla style, from behind rocks and bushes. They took a heavy toll on the army troops, who beat a hasty retreat.

Reluctant to fight at all, they scored one of the biggest Native American military victories ever against the U.S. Army.

The band members, many of them women and children, took their horses and belongings across the mountains of Idaho and north through Montana. They were close to the Canadian border when the army finally caught up with them and forced them back south. Only a few Nez Percé made it to Canada.

The band was sent to Leavenworth, Kansas, then to Oklahoma, then to the desert country of southeastern Washington state. There Chief Joseph died in 1904.

Noah Kellogg's Priceless Mule

· 1884 ·

The jackass story refuses to die, and certainly Noah Kellogg enjoyed telling it often enough.

Noah Kellogg was a carpenter by trade, drawn west to the mining boomtowns partly by the chance to practice his trade—in towns that rose seemingly overnight, carpenters always were in demand—and partly to look for gold. In 1883 he came to the latest hot mining territory—the Coeur d'Alene Mountains in northern Idaho. There he was put to work building flumes for underground mines in the Murray placer mining operation.

In his spare time Kellogg tried his own hand at prospecting. He wandered around the Coeur d'Alene River basin, always within a few miles of the town of Wallace, looking for the next big strike.

As a carpenter, he seemed a little more stable and reliable than some of the other gold rushers, and he rarely had much trouble raising money to continue the search. Once he persuaded two investors to pay for a month-long prospecting stint in the mountains west of Wallace. He returned home exhausted, his supplies gone, but with tools and mule still at the ready. He asked for more money to try again and got it.

What happened next no one has ever learned for sure.

Kellogg always maintained that one day, while he was walking through the mountains, he stopped to eat and then turned around to see where his pack animal was. The jackass was nearby, having knocked over a small pile of rocks, and was standing on top of an outcropping of bright, shiny metal. Kellogg went over to investigate.

It turned out not to be silver, just quartzite with galena mixed in; but it also turned out to be an indicator of other metal deposits.

Another story says that Kellogg had hooked up with a couple of other prospectors who put stories together and figured out where a large metal deposit could be found underground. According to this tale—repeated in lawsuits against Kellogg—the prospector was mostly trying to cheat his investors by his telling of the mule story.

In any event Kellogg hurried to the county clerk's office and filed his name as a witness on the land. That set off a huge run on the area, and Noah Kellogg wound up with little.

That was the story of the Coeur d'Alenes, which was not one of those mining districts in which lone miners could make a fortune independently. The district had been found in the hot summer of 1883 by two prospectors, Andrew Prichard and Bill Keeler, who'd spent a month scraping creek bottoms on the Coeur d'Alene River and then took several pounds of gold into a bar in Spokane, where they told anyone who would listen about their wonderful find. Within weeks, more than eight thousand prospectors were looking for precious metals in the district.

Although plenty of precious metals could be found in the area—including the largest supply of silver in the world—most of it was deep underground, and expensive underground mining, requiring heavy investment and many employees, was the only way to get at it. Large scale mines soon developed, like those that employed Noah Kellogg as a carpenter.

Kellogg's find led to one of the biggest of all the silver mines, Bunker Hill. The large mining operations became huge businesses, and the Coeur d'Alene River basin became known as the Silver Valley.

As for Noah Kellogg, his story finished in the old-style tradition of mining. After staking his claim, he was sued and sued again. He wound up with only a little money. He died in obscurity. The fate of his pack animal is unrecorded. But in Silver Valley legend at least, the story of his jackass lives on.

The Test Oath
· 1885 ·

They were a dozen men, all deputies of the U.S. marshal, and they were on a difficult mission.

They started in the Cache Valley, in the little town of Oxford—in the spring a lush and green oasis but now, in the middle of winter, deeply covered in snow. They were headed not on any road, but instead east, up over the high mountains, the northern reaches of the Wasatch, through thickly snowed-in forests. They did not want their targets to know of their approach.

So deep was the snow that they traveled mostly by bobsled, careening down mountainsides, barely avoiding injury. One of them had brought a thermometer, and they saw the temperature reach thirty degrees below zero. After four days, they had crossed the mountains and were overlooking the Bear Lake Valley. In it, just below them, was the little town of Paris, the county seat of Bear Lake County.

They had been on the move day and night, and as they saw the flickering lights of town below, it was still night. The group stopped, set up camp, carefully started a campfire, and cooked a meal. They rested until just before dawn. Then they headed down the mountainside and strode into town.

The men split up, heading to seven houses in town. They arrested the men in these houses, rousted from sleep in some cases, on charges of illegal cohabitation. Several were sent to jail.

This was only one of a series of raids. Another came at nearby Montpelier, when three deputies arrested several men on similar charges. In that case a crowd of local people gathered, surrounded the deputies, and freed the men, who were never identified.

Some of these arrests later brought convictions, which should not have been surprising. They were convicted not by their peers but by their political adversaries.

The deputies had been sent out by U.S. Marshal Fred T. Dubois, ordinarily a leader in the local Republican Party, but who the year before had organized a new political party called the Anti-Mormon Party. After the election of 1884, it controlled the Idaho legislature and passed a variety of new laws aimed at members of the Church of Jesus Christ of Latter-day Saints.

Dubois was among the growing number of people at the time who disapproved of the church's teachings allowing polygamy (a provision the church reversed a few years later). Besides that, most church members then were Democrats. Putting the two facts together, the Idaho territorial legislature passed a test oath law, which required voters to swear that they were not members of any church that taught what the Mormon Church taught. For a decade the law kept active Mormons from voting, serving on juries, or holding public office.

The law did not pass easily. When the bill got to the office of the territorial governor, William Bunn, he met with some of its backers, including Dubois, and said he was thinking about vetoing it. One of those men, Jim "Kentucky" Smith, walked up to him, pulled a gun from his pocket, and said, "Governor, you will not leave this room alive unless you sign it and sign it at once." He did.

One of the reasons the anti-Mormons acted so ferociously was that members of Congress had said Idaho would not become a state as long as Mormons had any influence there. With the test oath passed and Dubois's deputies sending to jail anyone who openly said they believed in the church's teachings, the stage was set for statehood. Dubois was elected to Congress in 1886, and three years later he helped push through the bill making Idaho a state. The test oath was repealed a few years after that.

Today, more than a fourth of Idaho's population consists of members of the Mormon Church. Its members have served in all of the state's highest offices.

But remnants of the past remain. Not until 1982 did the state finally, officially, repeal the section of the state constitution—long abandoned as a matter of practice—that kept Mormon Church members from voting or holding public office.

The Kleinschmidt Grade

· 1891 ·

"Don't look down!"

It was a serious admonition these road builders would give each other. Even those with the steadiest nerves could be thrown by a look straight down into Hells Canyon.

The crews of men working on the crazy Kleinschmidt project had to steel themselves every time they started work again. The work on the road was tough, as tough as any road building. They needed shovels to move dirt, pick axes to pry away rocks, and dynamite to blow through the larger, tougher obstacles. And there were plenty of those.

They were paid a dollar a day. It was good pay for the time, but this was unusual work. This wasn't just any road. These 22 miles were headed down the side of the deepest canyon gorge in North America—Hells Canyon.

They started from the top, where the mines were located—the mines that led crazy Albert Kleinschmidt to want to build this road in the first place. People had known for years about the copper in the mountains looming high overhead called the Seven Devils. But copper wasn't gold, and it wasn't remarkably valuable until electric power lines began to come into wide use. In 1885 Kleinschmidt, who had just made a pile of money mining copper in Montana, looked around for other reserves and settled on the Seven Devils country.

There he found plenty of copper and started what was called the Peacock Mine. But once he got it started, he discovered he had a problem. The Peacock Mine was located far from cities and roads. The nearest town was Council, more than 40 miles away, and nothing but thin trails ran from there to the mine. He didn't have the money to build a railroad on his own, and stages wouldn't be able to haul the heavy copper.

What was so frustrating was that three thousand feet down below the mines was a great, navigable river—the Snake River. Boats could haul away the copper if only he could connect the mines up in the mountains with the river. But the grade was extremely steep.

In the end he decided to spend twenty thousand dollars to build a road headed down the side of the canyon.

In 1889 he hired crews of road builders, some of them experienced men who had built roads over tough terrain before, and set them to work on the side of the mountain. Moving steadily down the hill, developing switchbacks and trying to keep the grades gentle, they worked through the seasons.

Two years later the road was built. After all that, it never carried a pound of copper ore. Steamboats trying to reach the road from the river had difficulty negotiating the landing; there was no good place to put in nearby, and the currents were treacherous. Before those problems could be solved, the financial panic of 1893 hit, and copper prices plummeted. The Seven Devils Mines were nearly closed. A few years later, with the panic over, they were again operating at full strength, but Kleinschmidt had bailed out, and the new investors decided to build a railroad from Council to the mines. When prices fell again, the railroad was abandoned, and the mines scaled back their operations, this time for good.

The Kleinschmidt road is still there, is maintained, and still used. Engineers have remarked that it is a well-designed road. A passenger car is reported to have used it in 1909, and adventurous drivers still do.

Riots in the Coeur d'Alene

· 1892 ·

Hot, dusty, and noisy—this meeting of the Miners Union of the Coeur d'Alenes was seething even before the union's secretary, Leon Allison, strode into the big, wooden meeting room.

These were angry miners. Accustomed to working ten-hour days in horrific conditions, where temperatures rose into triple digits, humidity surpassed that of the rain forest, and injuries were frequent, they had drawn the line when it came to pay—they wanted $3.50 a day, no less. Some miners were still working, but many others had been replaced by out-of-state "scabs" who would work for considerably less. Allison had been fired a couple of weeks earlier by his shift boss for getting involved with the union, and there were plenty of others like him. The out-of-work miners were primed to do . . . something.

Allison stepped up to the podium with the other union officers and looked out at the crowd. The noise level settled; as it did, he heard something that chilled his bones.

Back toward the far end of the meeting room, he saw a man he'd met once before, in Nevada—Black Jack Griffin, a miner. Griffin yelled out at the crowd, "I know that man! He's not one of you! He's a company goon! He's a Pinkerton!"

Allison sucked in his breath. "I am not," he said. "I've been here the better part of a year, working the mines just like you.

And who is this guy anyway? Just coming up here from Nevada, and now he wants to throw suspicion on your union officers?"

The meeting erupted. Miners yelled at each other, desperate to find out if they had a spy in their midst. They did.

Leon Allison was in fact Charles Angelo Siringo, one of the most skilled operatives of the Pinkerton Detective Agency, which in those days was employed by many mine owners to bust unions attempting to start up. For months Siringo had been working undercover, sending daily reports to the mine owners association. He kept a Colt .45 under one arm and a sharp Bowie knife strapped to his leg, just in case.

Siringo, sensing his life was in danger, kept a low profile the next few days, ducking in and out of the little mining town of Gem. When they spotted him entering the boarding house where he lived, a group of armed union members prepared to ambush him when he emerged. Siringo, however, had a fine instinct for survival. He cut a hole in the floor of his room, crawled underneath the boarding house and under the boardwalk along Gem's main, and only, street, and escaped into the forest.

The miners were enraged when they realized he'd gotten away. Union members marched to the nearest mine, exchanged gunfire with the guards there, then blew up several buildings with dynamite. They marched about sixty "scabs" from the mine to the meeting hall at gunpoint, then put them on a train bound out of state. Next, some four hundred men gathered and rode flatcars to the mines near Kellogg, seized mining concentrator equipment at a half-dozen mines, and promised to blow them all up unless the mine owners gave in to the union's terms. They did, and miners cheered in the streets for days.

That was not the end of the story. State and federal troops, about 1,500 strong, were ordered into the Silver Valley, and hundreds of men associated with the union activities were rounded up. They were kept outdoors, in what was called "The Bullpen," for more than two months without anyone bringing charges against them. Most were later released.

But the poisoned relations between labor and management would last a long time. It would lead to many more years of unrest, of violence, and even the assassination of an Idaho governor.

Today, the Silver Valley is a quieter place. Almost all of the mines are gone; just two remain in operation.

Butch Cassidy at
Montpelier
· 1896 ·

The clock on the wall showed that three in the afternoon was just about to toll, and for cashier E. C. Gray that meant the Bank of Montpelier was about to close for the day.

As he always did at about this time, Gray closed the window blinds and began to shoo some of the customers out of the bank. They'd been hanging around to talk a little business and gossip. There were four of them lounging in the bank to escape the summer heat and one, William Perkins, was a city council member, so gossip was flowing freely. Gray and his assistant, Bud McIntosh, had had a busy day, and there was much bookkeeping yet to be done. The Bank of Montpelier was not large, but it was proud: It held Idaho state bank charter Number 1.

Gray didn't know that two men were about to step into his bank and make his daily bookkeeping useless.

The day was August 13. The weather was hot, the sky almost cloudless, and the air muggy. Montpelier is just north of Bear Lake, and some of the lake's water had become airborne in the heat. The local farmers and stockmen were out in their fields, cutting hay and watering stock, taking advantage of the back end of summer before the harsh late fall and winter would shut down everything in the area. The divided city— split down Washington Street with Mormons on one side and

Gentiles on the other, a remnant of the way the city had grown from its early days as a railroad stop—was quiet, with only light traffic.

In fact Montpelier was so quiet and unworldly that when three horsemen, with a small sorrel pack mare trailing behind, rode slowly through town, they were noticed right off for the relative finery of their clothes and mounts.

The three men stopped in front of the bank. Two of them entered; the third dismounted and took the four horses around to the back of the building.

Inside the bank, the two men surveyed the scene and pulled their guns, moving quickly and efficiently. The leader, a stocky blond man, stayed just to the side of the front door, keeping watch on the room. He spoke in a cool voice and was fast with his instructions: "Put your hands up and keep your mouths shut." He then told the customers to face the nearest wall and keep their hands in the air. They all complied.

His partner, a taller and darker man, stepped behind the cashier desk where Bud McIntosh was working. The robber produced a sack and ordered McIntosh to dump all the available paper money into it. McIntosh paused—a big mistake—then went for the Winchester rifle that had been placed nearby for just such an emergency robbery situation. It was to no avail: The tall robber clobbered him on the forehead with a revolver.

The robber made a quick move to hit him again, but his partner at the door told him to stop. "Just get the money," he said.

The tall robber did as he was told. Into a second bag, one of the bank's own money bags, he put a pile of gold coins, some of which had been sitting on the counter in plain view to prove to customers that the bank was solvent. The robber grabbed a stack of silver coins, as well.

Now the leader started moving through the room, toward the back door. He helped his partner with the heavy bags and told the people in the room—Gray, McIntosh, and the four customers—that they would not be harmed as long as they kept still and quiet for ten minutes. Then he and his partner vanished out the back.

The men inside waited and listened carefully. They could tell that four horses were casually riding away. Once the sound had faded, they made their move, telegraphing Bear Lake County Sheriff Jeff Davis at the city of Paris, about 10 miles away.

Davis was at the bank within an hour. He quickly found out that there had been three robbers and rounded up a posse to pursue them. The robbers had a head start, but Gray and McIntosh weren't worried: They had an idea who the robbers were and, thus, where they likely were headed. Plus, Gray had his bank insured against daylight robbery.

Everyone in Montpelier was familiar with Tom McCarty, a well-known, veteran bank robber. McCarty and his gang had only recently spent a winter at Star Valley, just across the state line in Wyoming, and they had so charmed the community there that they were made welcome. In fact two of the gang members eloped with young women from Star Valley, and McCarty quietly married his fiancée in Montpelier. Gray and others in town had talked about it for months, happy with the fact that prosperous little Montpelier had been attractive to a hard-bitten bank robber. They figured that because McCarty was so well known in Montpelier, he wouldn't try to rob its bank. On August 13, Gray and Davis assumed they had figured wrong.

Actually, they were right.

Davis led one posse, then another, east to the nearby Wyoming line and probed around in his search for the trio. At one point they spotted a sorrel mare wandering around by herself, but they failed to catch her when they gave chase. They searched through places where McCarty and his gang had been and seemed likely to go, including the Star Valley. They found little.

Soon the trail went cold, but not before Davis, who heard talk about a trio of ranch hands in Wyoming who had vanished just a couple of days before the Montpelier stickup, began to piece together who was actually behind the robbery. He compared descriptions of the Montpelier robbers with the McCarty gang and found they didn't match: Ages and physical descriptions were too different. Then he began to think about who these robbers really might be. He came to a new conclusion: This was a Butch Cassidy stickup.

One key piece of evidence was the leader's reluctance to engage in violence unless absolutely necessary. Butch knew that legal statutes of limitation for bank robberies ran out long before those for murder. The tall man with him in the bank had been Elza Lay, and the holder of the horses at the back of the bank was Bob Meeks, brand new to the world of bank robbery.

Apart from making a living robbing banks, Cassidy had a specific need for this money, which was carried by the pack mare taking its own route, sometimes miles from the three robbers on the lam. So did Lay and Meeks. The three were friends of a fellow bandit named Matt Warner, who was in jail in Utah on what was ironically a trumped-up murder charge. Most of the Montpelier money, estimated at more than sixteen thousand dollars, went to hire the best Utah lawyers available, and Warner wound up with a relatively short prison term.

Cassidy apparently never returned to Idaho, but Meeks did—and not of his own free will. He was passing through Cheyenne, Wyoming, when a railroad detective recognized him as someone who might have been involved with a railroad robbery. Meeks was able to supply an alibi for that charge, but his alibi placed him close to Montpelier around the time of the bank robbery. Alfred Budge, the Bear Lake County prosecutor, got hold of this information and crafted a case against Meeks. He was tried in Idaho, where Gray testified against him, admitting that he hadn't actually seen him inside the bank. Budge, who would go on to serve on the Idaho Supreme Court, won a conviction against Meeks, and late in 1897, Meeks was sent to the Idaho State Penitentiary in Boise.

Meeks became a notorious prisoner, attempting escape twice and losing a leg on the second occasion, when he was shot. Released in 1912, he apparently wandered to Colorado and took a job as a ranch manager.

Elza Lay was eventually imprisoned for another robbery in New Mexico but later became a businessman and an investor in oil properties. He lived quietly until his death in 1933.

The Bank of Montpelier survived until 1925, when "unfounded rumors" in town caused its collapse. The building was later taken over by Montgomery Ward.

The ultimate fate of Butch Cassidy is not positively known. Most historians believe he went to South America with a gunman he later hooked up with named Harry Longabaugh (or possibly Lombaugh), better known as the "Sundance Kid," and died in a shoot-out in Bolivia.

The Trial of Diamondfield Jack

· 1902 ·

The sheepherder was working his flock around the edges of the rugged City of Rocks natural area when he saw something that stunned him—two of his fellow sheepherders lying dead amid the rocks, shot to death. He looked around and hurried to the nearest town, Albion, to report the killings. It was more than civic duty. He was worried about his personal safety—he had heard Diamondfield Jack was back in the area and that meant his life was at risk.

The sheriff thought the same thing and began an immediate search for Jack. More than a year later, he found him in a jail in Yuma, Arizona. Jack and his partner, Fred Gleason, who was arrested in Montana, were brought back to Albion to stand trial for murder.

They had reason to suspect "Diamondfield" Jackson Lee Davis. A solid, serious-looking man with a thick handlebar mustache, he got his nickname from his fruitless searching for diamonds all over the West. After years of making little headway, he joined with Gleason and became a hired gun.

These were the days of bitter conflict between cattlemen and sheepmen throughout the American West. When the cattlemen around Oakley, Idaho, especially the wealthy John Sparks, concluded that sheepmen were sending flocks too close to their land and ruining their grazing fields, Diamond-field Jack was brought in to "persuade" the sheepmen to move elsewhere. The persuasion was not always gentle.

After wounding one sheepherder, Jack rode south into Nevada until things cooled down. After a couple of months, he returned to Idaho, and not long after that the two dead sheep-men were found. By that time Jack had disappeared again.

Although the case against Diamondfield Jack was based only on circumstantial evidence, it was quickly taken up by an ambitious Boise attorney named William Borah. John Sparks and the other cattlemen hired Idaho's veteran criminal law at-torney James Hawley to defend Jack. The trial started in Albion in April 1897, and Jack's legal troubles would last for five years. He was eventually convicted (though Gleason, who was tried separately, was acquitted) of murder and sentenced to be hanged. Twice the scheduled time for the hanging drew so close that crowds had begun to gather in downtown Albion to watch, only to see messengers frantically ride into town with a reprieve.

Then, in October 1898, one of the foremen at the largest cattle ranch in the area, Jim Bower, walked into a state pardons board meeting and said that he and a co-worker, Jeff Gray, had encountered the two sheepmen and had killed them in self-defense. Bower and Gray were tried and found to have done the deed, but in self-defense, and were released. However, Dia-mondfield Jack remained in jail and eventually was transferred to the state prison, and he remained scheduled for execution.

Finally, in 1902, after the case had taken several trips to both the Idaho and United States Supreme Court, the state par-dons board voted two to one to release Jack. On December 18, 1902, Jack walked out of the state prison just east of Boise. He headed down a dusty road to the Boise natatorium, a big swimming and recreation building, and there had a few drinks with his attorney, James Hawley, who had just been elected mayor of Boise. Then he took a train to Tonopah, Nevada.

William Borah went on to become a United States senator, and Hawley later served as governor of Idaho; they would join forces only a few years later in another big trial, that of "Big Bill" Haywood, a labor radical. John Sparks moved to Nevada and became governor of that state.

And Diamondfield Jack? He stayed for years in Tonopah, finally making a fortune in a gold mining company and then losing it, and spent his last years, until his death in 1949, wandering across the American West.

The Magic Valley
·1903·

Ira Burton Perrine had reason to be discouraged as he trudged south toward the big rip in the land and stared down into the Snake River canyon, hundreds of feet below. His plans to get rich in the West just weren't working out very well, and this place to which he'd been directed seemed to hold little promise.

The course of the rest of his life, though, was about to change. And not only that—I. B. Perrine would change not only his life but this land—as if by magic.

Up to this point, little had been magical. He was one of eleven children raised on a farm in Indiana. His parents wanted him to become a minister. Perrine rejected that idea and in the early 1880s headed to the hottest mining country in the West, Idaho's Wood River Valley, to make his fortune. Once he got there, the mining bosses told him he was too small to work in the mines.

Determined not to give up, he raised money to buy dairy cows, planning to sell milk to the miners. He drove the cows into the middle of the Wood River Valley, only to discover there were no grazing lands for them. With his cows starving and he himself losing money and growing desperate, Perrine asked the locals where he could graze his cattle. There were no obvious answers. To the north lay mountains; to the south lay desert growing little more than sagebrush for hundreds of miles.

Then a friend, Charles Walgamott, told him about a place along the Snake River, about 70 miles to the south. Perrine drove the cattle south and finally came to the ledge overlooking the canyon. He could see green places—plants growing down by the river. But most of the land around was still barren. How could someone make a living here? After feeding his cattle and settling down for a while in the area, which he called Blue Lakes, Ira Perrine began to come up with an astonishing variety of answers to that question.

One story has it that he saw a vision of what was to come—a rich farm valley with brand new cities and towns. Whatever the case, he mostly forgot mining and started instead growing crops, and he soon found that the volcanic soil was actually excellent for farming when it was irrigated. He grew crops usually associated with southern states: cotton and tobacco, peaches, apples and plums, and nut trees. He maintained a big orchard. It survived partly because the high canyon walls protected it during the winters. His crops won prizes, even an international award at a Paris exposition in 1900.

But that was only the beginning. Perrine knew that he and other farmers could do the same thing on the vast desert lands above the canyon if there were only a way to bring water up there from the Snake River. Then he saw his opportunity. It came in 1894 in a tucked-away provision of the Sundry Civil Appropriations Bill passed by Congress that year. The provision, called the Carey Act, allowed up to a million acres of land to be transferred from the federal government to the states and to private citizens if the land were to be irrigated and "reclaimed" from the desert. Idaho was the second state to take advantage of the new law. More specifically, Ira Perrine took advantage of it.

Perrine gathered together a group of businessmen—Frank Buhl, Stanley Milner, and Peter Kimberly among them, with help from Idaho politician Frank Gooding—to organize and finance the project of bringing water up the canyon, then buying and selling newly irrigated land. These projects were well under-way by 1900, and within another year, Perrine had laid out the tracts for a new city only miles from his old Blue Lakes farm. Soon that city—with Perrine one of the major owners in the new business community—was founded and growing fast. It was called Twin Falls, after the two Snake River waterfalls nearby.

A century later, it's all still there. The land Perrine set up for transition from desert to farm is farmland still, and the area is called the Magic Valley due to its amazing transition from hopeless desert to rich, irrigated farmland. Twin Falls is the re-gional business center, and many of the other cities in the area—Buhl, Kimberly, Hollister, Gooding—are named for Per-rine's associates.

Across the Snake River, just north of Twin Falls, is a long, high bridge called the I. B. Perrine Bridge. From it, if you look at the right angle, you can see the Blue Lakes, where a dream, and the magic, began.

Assassination

· 1905 ·

On the last Saturday of 1905, which turned out to be the last day of his life, Frank Steunenberg was not much inclined to leave his Caldwell home.

The reason wasn't that he wasn't inclined to work. He was known as a hard worker at his newspaper, banking, and ranching businesses. It wasn't because he wasn't sociable; he had been twice elected governor of Idaho—in 1896 he won the highest percentage of the vote by anyone ever running for that office in the state—and was thinking about running for office again.

Part of it may have been his exhausting trip during most of the week before to his sheep ranch near Bliss. Part of it may have been the snow and the cold. Snow was falling hard early that morning, and it picked up as the day went on; more than six inches had fallen by early evening. It seemed a good day to huddle indoors. Steunenberg's children were all home—one was back on Christmas vacation from college at Walla Walla, Washington—and Frank was of a mind to spend the day enjoying his family.

But around noon a visitor upset his plans. He was an agent of the New York Life Insurance Company, and he had come to warn Steunenberg that his life insurance policy, not yet re-signed, was scheduled to end with the year, little more than a day away. He had to renew now to keep it in force. Could he meet with Steunenberg at his bank later that afternoon? Reluctantly, the ex-governor agreed.

Steunenberg sloshed downtown—it was within easy walking distance—through deep snow and over boarded sidewalks, to sign the papers at the bank and then to relax a bit in the lobby of the Saratoga Hotel. Then, darkness having fallen and the snow continuing to do likewise, he made his way back home.

His yard was fenced and a gate had been built in front of his house. When Steunenberg pulled the wooden latch to open it, and then closed it again, an explosion erupted, an explosion that rocked the Steunenberg household and was heard all over town. Dynamite had been attached to the gate. The former governor died within hours.

The assassin was collared quickly. He was Harry Orchard (also known as Albert Horsley and Thomas Hogan), a former miner who had been active in the labor unions of northern Idaho's Silver Valley and who worked with many of the men who were sworn enemies of Steunenberg. The former governor had generated loud criticism among labor leaders during his time in office for his crackdown on union activity in the Silver Valley in 1898, even invoking martial law and suspending some civil liberties.

Many Idahoans wondered if Orchard had accomplices within labor organizations. Many of Idaho's leaders, including Governor Frank Gooding, thought he did. Under pressure, Orchard fingered several other labor leaders who he said had put him up to the deed. Private detectives from Idaho seized three nationally prominent labor leaders in Denver, including the highly controversial "Big Bill" Haywood, and brought them to Boise for trial.

It became Idaho's trial of the century. The prosecutors included a future Idaho senator, William Borah, and governor, James Hawley. The defense attorneys included the nationally renowned Clarence Darrow, then building his reputation as one of the country's foremost trial lawyers. At a time when spellbinding oratory was not unusual in major trials, the Haywood trial at the sweltering Ada County courthouse set new standards. It was a spectacular trial, watched nationally in the newspapers (and attended by flocks of reporters), and it made the reputations of many of its participants.

After three months, Haywood and the others were acquitted, but debate went on—and goes on today—about whether they in fact engineered the assassination.

Harry Orchard was sentenced to death, but after a declaration that he had become a devout Christian, the state pardons board commuted the sentence to life imprisonment. Orchard became a trustee at the Idaho State Penitentiary, where he tended a garden and kept chickens until his death there in 1954 at the age of eighty-eight.

Today, a statue of Steunenberg stands in front of and faces the Idaho capitol building in Boise.

Fire of the Century
·1910·

In 1910 Wallace was a tough mining town familiar with hardships and danger. Its young mayor, the attorney Walter Hanson, thought its people would not easily be persuaded to evacuate. But the young man was beginning to think that the time to vacate the town had arrived.

The summer had been tense. Ever since June, small fires were popping up everywhere in the forest country of northern Idaho. The winter before had been dry, and the summer was miserably hot, one of the hottest ever. The fires all around multiplied; then wind, and occasional lightning storms, made it worse. Finally, President William Taft even sent in federal troops to help with firefighting.

At Wallace, a small town in a narrow valley blocked in by high mountains on the north and south, the skies were turning gray and then darkening because of smoke and debris in the air. Cinders began to fall in the streets.

On this day, August 21, the sky fell so dark that the street lights were lit at three o'clock in the afternoon. Mayor Hanson left his downtown law office and walked a couple of blocks to talk to a man who might be able to tell him if his town was about to burn to the ground.

He was William Weigle, the national forest supervisor in charge of the firefighting effort. Weigle had no certain answer. One of the worst fires, in nearby Placer Canyon, had been fed by the wind, and there were no large crews nearby to stop it. And the men in the area were running out of supplies.

He told Hanson, "God only knows what's going to happen next. I don't."

After Hanson left, Weigle set off for the mountains to find out what he could. He reached Placer Canyon, calmer now, and climbed up the nearby mountainside. It was then, at about four in the afternoon—with the sky as dark as late twilight— that the wind stopped. An eerie calm settled over the mountain peaks.

For a moment Weigle relaxed. If the wind was dying, the fires would be a lot easier to manage. Then it occurred to him that he was standing in the only calm spot, like the eye of a hurricane.

Weigle hurried back down the mountain toward Wallace but stopped when a man named "Speedy" Swift met him. Swift had just been in town to see a doctor—he was still sick but also worried about his wife and baby up in the mountains, maybe trapped by fire. Weigle told him he would go up and get them and sent Swift back to town. Weigle found them, just as their ranch was about to be surrounded by fire, and sent them to town.

Then he started uphill again, and just as he did the wind kicked up—nearly to tornado strength—and he was nearly surrounded by fire himself. At one point he had to crawl into an old mining tunnel while fires raged above.

When he finally ducked out of the tunnel, he could see fire headed down the mountain, straight for Wallace.

In town he found Hanson trying to pour water on his house, a nearby hospital, and whatever other buildings he could. The two men got to work evacuating as many people as they could.

The fire reached Wallace, but the city was luckier than it might have been—just a third of the town burned, and the rest, including the downtown area, was spared. It was the largest community actually burned by the fire.

But the great fire of 1910 was much bigger than it appeared to one community. It raged all over northern Idaho and western Montana, south to Wyoming, and north into Canada. The smoke from the fires was so thick and heavy it migrated nearly to the East Coast and even darkened skies in Toronto, Canada.

Nearly a century later, the Idaho legislature considered a resolution on a proposal to improve elk habitat in the Clearwater River country in north central Idaho. Experts agreed that the decline in the elk population and the problems with their living conditions in that area could be traced back to the disastrous fire of 1910.

America's First Jewish Governor
·1914·

When Moses Alexander came to Boise in 1894, he took over an empty business space that had been occupied by a saloon. Following his trade, he turned it into a men's clothing store. A little more than two decades later, when he became governor of Idaho, he told the Idaho legislature, "The licensed saloon has no longer a right of existence in our state." He spent the next two years making good on that statement, and in 1916 he pushed through a constitutional amendment imposing prohibition in Idaho, several years before it happened nationally.

Even before that, he pushed through a bill banning the sale of alcohol in Idaho, and received a death threat in return: "If you sign bill no 142, you will be killed. You know that the people of Idaho don't want prohibition. Don't take this as a joke." He signed it anyway, and no assassination plot was ever uncovered.

He had campaigned on a platform of prohibition—that, and honest government. Just weeks before the 1914 election for governor, the state treasurer was caught with his fingers in the safe; he and his chief deputy were accused, and soon after convicted, of stealing more than $93,000 of state money. Although the Republican governor, John Haines, had moved quickly to have the treasurer arrested and the state reimbursed by insurers, the scandal had hurt him and swayed the vote to Alexander.

What people knew, but didn't much discuss in that election of 1914, was the reason it has been so noted in history books ever since: Moses Alexander was Jewish, and in 1914 he became the first Jewish governor of an American state.

It was not a fact that was likely to be a big political benefit. Idaho's Jewish population, never large, was especially small in those days, and almost nonexistent outside Boise. But Alexander had arrived in Boise politically adept and experienced.

Born in Bavaria, he lived for a time in New York City—learning the men's clothing trade and becoming a top salesperson—before moving on to take over a store in Chillecothe, Ohio. There he was elected to the city council and next became mayor. Restless once again, he planned to move to Alaska because of the gold boom there but settled instead midway between Ohio and Alaska, in Boise, Idaho, where he considered his long-term prospects to be better. The men's clothing store he opened in Boise, at 9th and Idaho Streets, stayed in business more than a century, and spawned more stores in southern Idaho and eastern Oregon. The building still stands.

There was no Jewish congregation in Boise when he arrived; Alexander quickly took the lead in organizing one and also built a synagogue, the Beth Israel. The congregation he began still meets today.

Boise was in a mood to leave its more raucous pioneer days behind and become a stable community, and Alexander shared the view and led the charge. He ran for mayor of Boise, as a Democrat in a Republican town, and was easily elected twice. He pushed through new, "progressive" reform legislation, shutting down saloons and limiting (he couldn't quite yet eliminate) the activities of prostitutes in the city.

These became his cornerstones as he ran for governor, narrowly losing one election and then, in 1914, beating an incumbent Republican governor in a mostly Republican year in Idaho.

Nationally, Jewish organizations sent letters and made public statements about their pleasure in Alexander's election. One of these pronouncements, from nearby Spokane, Washington, said: "Every Jew rejoices with you, both in the fact that you have won and how you have won, for it is well known that you stood loyally in heart and expression, not only as a true servant of the people, but as a Jew."

Moses Alexander, a leader of crusades against the sale of alcohol and for economic development, himself had little to say on the subject. He served two terms as governor and then went back to his business. He died in Boise in 1932.

Famous Potatoes
· 1917 ·

Joe Marshall was proud of his potatoes; he was a guy who did nothing halfway. Though he was on a remote farm in south central Idaho, far from any big city, raising an obscure crop along with only a few other farmers in the region—only twenty-five thousand acres were planted in potatoes in Idaho in 1917—he was convinced that the potatoes grown on the flat Snake River Plain were the best in the world.

He just had to make everyone else see it that way.

Potato farming was hard work. Marshall planted and dug his potatoes out of the rocky soil, which was difficult because the field was strewn with debris from lava flows in some places. He planted at a variety of locations around southern Idaho: Jerome, Aberdeen, Declo. One year he tried planting at higher elevations in eastern Idaho, around Ashton and in the Teton Valley, where the growing season was short. Even there he got good results, especially once he started growing Russett Burbanks. He packed his potatoes in bags bearing the label "Blue Diamond."

In the wake of these successes, Joe Marshall grew increasingly frustrated. He was growing some of the best potatoes around, but he got the same low prices as potato farmers everywhere else, and his potatoes were mixed in with other varieties. He decided to do something about it.

In those days the big market for potato sales was Chicago. The national potato brokers were there, and for years they'd been buying his Blue Diamond label potatoes. But as he strode the sidewalks of downtown Chicago and finally turned into one of the Tofanetti's restaurants in the financial district, he was about to try something new.

Joe Marshall was out of place in downtown Chicago. He had grown up in a log cabin in rural Ohio, a building so rickety that snow often blew through the cracks in the walls while he slept. He moved west and worked on a series of farms, never in a city. He was not a top business executive or financial analyst. But he knew something about selling.

Marshall spoke to the manager at Tofanetti's and held up his big bag of Blue Diamond potatoes, only days out of the Idaho fields. He held up a single potato. It was bigger than most potatoes the cooks there had seen, better shaped, and it felt better. He cut one open; it was like meal, not soggy the way so many potatoes were. He had them cook a few. They tasted better; they had better texture; and they looked better on the plate.

Marshall offered to sell them as many as they wanted for $1.40 per one-hundred-pound sack—more than three times as much as a broker would have given him. The restaurant manager snapped up the potatoes and, with money now on the line, began promoting his potatoes as special Idaho potatoes.

Before long the whole Tofanetti's chain began doing the same thing, and within months other restaurants in Chicago, then Milwaukee, climbed aboard. Word spread around the country as diners said they wanted these fluffy, tasty potatoes instead of the soggy, tasteless ones they often were served. Menus were redesigned to highlight "Idaho Potatoes!"

No longer would Marshall allow his potatoes to be dumped in with everyone else's. He was growing a special kind of potato, he said, and he demanded a premium price for them.

Marshall began to prosper—one of the few Idaho farmers who did over the next few years. Just a few years later, in the farm depression that followed World War I, many Idaho farms began to fail financially, and several banks asked Marshall to take over management of many of them. He began raising and selling his potatoes on some of these farms as well, expanding his marketing even wider.

In 1937 Marshall helped create the Idaho Potato Commission, which was responsible for marketing Idaho potatoes. It advertised nationally about the wonders of the Idaho potato, and soon supermarkets as well as restaurants were labeling Idaho potatoes as such—and charging more for them.

Idaho and the potato have been closely identified with each other ever since. Even now, Idaho's car license plates carry the words *Famous Potatoes*.

But they are famous mostly because of one man's astonishing marketing savvy.

The Creation of Sun Valley

·1936·

The call to Averell Harriman, chairman of the board of Union Pacific Railroad, would have been the stuff of comedy if it hadn't been half expected. Here he was, an American business tycoon, hearing his secretary tell him that an Austrian count was calling from somewhere in the Rocky Mountain states. And when he picked up the phone, he heard an excited voice saying: "I've found it! Come and see for yourself!"

Harriman did, taking the railroad out from New York to Idaho with his friend Bill Paley, the chairman of the Columbia Broadcasting System radio network. Both of them concluded Count Felix Schaffgotsch was exactly right: This spot in the middle of Idaho where the Snake River Plain bumped into the Sawtooth Mountains was just the place for America's first major ski resort. It had the right kind of snow; it was sunny most of the time; and the areas at the base of the mountains were protected from the heavy winds found in so much of the American West.

"What he'd found was glorious," Harriman recalled years later. "Powder snow over open slopes, with Bald Mountain close at hand. By unanimous agreement the place was called Sun Valley. It named itself."

Harriman, who was the son of a previous Union Pacific chairman, was eager to build. He had often vacationed in Europe, where skiing was a favored pastime before it was barely known at all in the United States. The few places available for skiing in America were poorly developed. Most of the skiing places in eastern states were too icy, he recalled, and hardly any place to ski existed in the West.

Harriman saw a country just then climbing out of economic depression, and he wanted his railroad to do something different and exciting. He sent an acquaintance, Count Felix, west to look for a good spot for skiing that also happened to be located close to Union Pacific tracks. His intent was to link the skiing resort to the East via Union Pacific.

Later, Harriman said of the count's tour: "The railroad organization took hold of him and steered him around, so he wasn't on a Lewis and Clark expedition." But he traveled widely and considered and rejected a long list of places well known among skiers in the years since: Aspen, Colorado; Lake Tahoe, Nevada; Alta, Utah; Jackson, Wyoming; and many more.

The count toured Idaho along with a local Union Pacific representative but found nothing worth reporting and headed back to Colorado to revisit another location. After he'd left, the Union Pacific representative headed to the Hotel Boise for a beer. He bumped into the head of the state highway department and told him about the count's quest.

The state official asked him, "Did you show him the Ketchum area? That might be a possibility." The company man hadn't, but he immediately thought it was a good idea and hurriedly recalled the count to Idaho. They set off for Ketchum.

A main Union Pacific line ran across southern Idaho, but at Shoshone a spur ran north up into the Wood River Valley, where some mining operations still existed near Ketchum and Hailey. On the count's recommendation, Sun Valley would be located at the very end of that spur.

Sun Valley ski resort would feature the world's first chair-lifts (designed by railroad technicians) as well as a lodge, a wide range of entertainment facilities, and a small community made to look, as Harriman said, like an Austrian mountain village. It quickly became famous. Movies were made there, and celebrities visited the area, including Ernest Hemingway, who liked to fish in Silver Creek, a few miles south.

Today, Sun Valley is Idaho's best-known vacation spot, and its skiing quality—as Count Felix probably would have predicted—often ranks at or near the top among ski resorts nationally.

Feeding the Army
· 1941 ·

J. R. Simplot had just gotten his rapidly expanding business under some control when, on a pleasant spring day, he received a group of visitors and his world changed forever.

They were from the U.S. Army Quartermaster Corps. They wanted to talk with Simplot about supplying large—really large—amounts of dehydrated potatoes, something no one had ever done before.

"We need good food that's nutritious, will last a long time, can be easily transported, and can be used a variety of ways," he was told. The United States was sending food to Great Britain as part of the Lend-Lease program, and potatoes would be needed for that. In addition the Army officers were preparing for the likelihood that eventually they would be called into the war escalating in Europe, and they would quickly need large amounts of food for the troops. Food supplies were among the items they wanted to line up now, before the crisis hit.

Could Simplot supply the massive amount of dehydrated potatoes that the army and other organizations would need over the next few years? "Sure," he said. J. R. Simplot rarely hesitated when it came time to make a critical business decision. Then he set out to figure out how to do it.

He had reason for confidence, because he had done the same thing with onions six months earlier.

Simplot had for fourteen years been in the business of raising, sorting, and shipping potatoes and onions, having started his business from scratch in Declo, Idaho, during the Great Depression. He dropped out of school in the eighth grade and took work wherever he could find it, but at the same time, he worked to establish his own business.

He seemed to jump at every good opportunity before settling on potato and onion production as his main business. In 1940 he visited a processor to whom he'd been selling onions and who was now late in making payments for them. In the processor's office, he met a customer of that processor, equally dissatisfied, who had not received dehydrated onions on time. At that moment Simplot offered to sell dehydrated onions to him directly. The fact that he didn't know how to do it—yet—didn't matter. He would learn.

He was successful enough at doing it to come to the attention of the army. Though it had grown rapidly, Simplot's company was still relatively small and regional, but it was expanding into areas of great interest to army suppliers.

After Simplot told the Army officers he'd supply their dehydrated potatoes and signed a contract, he pulled together his key employees and they developed a new mechanical process for dehydrating potatoes in mass quantities. Faced with the problem of peeling such massive amounts of potatoes, they devised a new process for softening the potato skins in order to remove them.

Production grew bigger and bigger. During World War II, Simplot supplied almost a third of the potatoes bought by the U.S. military. They were not always pretty. The early potatoes often looked gray or brown (a problem he later corrected). But they were nutritious and gave the army what it needed.

After the war, Simplot moved into frozen french fry production and still later became a primary potato supplier for the McDonalds fast-food chain.

The J. R. Simplot Company, now based in Boise, has continued to expand over the years, across many states and overseas. Simplot himself has become involved with a wide range of businesses. He provided the key financing for, and for years took an active role in, what is now Idaho's largest business, Micron Technology, which produces computer microchips and related products.

Simplot has become a billionaire, Idaho's richest resident.

Nuclear Energy Lights Arco

· 1955 ·

People in the little town of Arco were holding their breath because what was about to happen had never happened before. It was a cool July night in the high desert. Dark had fallen only a couple of hours before, and they were on the threshold of a new era. That night, some of them knew what was happening; the rest would know the next day.

Some watched the lights.

Eighteen miles east of Arco, a man prepared to flip a switch. The man was Ray Haroldsen, a native of the Idaho Falls area, and at eleven o'clock on the night of July 17, 1955, he turned a switch and made history.

For months he and his co-workers had been at work at an advanced and tightly secured federal facility out in the bleak eastern Idaho desert. They were working on a project called BORAX III—Boiling Water Reactor Experiment. Their intent was to use nuclear energy to do something it had never done before: generate electric power.

Nuclear energy facilities were not new to this remote desert land. Their history went back to the creation of the Atomic Energy Commission in 1946 and its decision that the federal government needed a testing area for nuclear reactors. They thought a relatively remote location would be a wise choice for conducting their experiments and dithered between

Montana and eastern Idaho sites before choosing Idaho. Several reactor testing stations were built in the desert near Arco in the next few years.

In 1951 Experimental Breeder Reactor-1 was built in the flat lands about 50 miles west of Idaho Falls. It became the first nuclear reactor ever to produce nuclear energy, but initially it was not hooked up to anything. Eventually, several of the federal operations out in the desert would be supplied with the nuclear-produced electric power.

Nuclear energy was viewed cautiously, as the researchers investigated their options and the problems each presented. One of the tests resulted in water shooting 50 to 150 feet above one of the reactor tanks, looking like a geyser. "Yes, we knew about hazards at that time," said one of the researchers later.

Almost four years passed before scientists and administrators decided to go public with their new technology. Then they decided to see if they could light up Arco with the electricity they were generating. But there were more difficulties. They needed cooperation from the local electric utility, Utah Power and Light (UP&L), to coordinate and "match speeds" on their power supply so the right amount of electricity, and a continuous supply of it, would go to Arco. At just the right moment, the UP&L electric supply to the town would have to be cut off. They had a hard time finding the right transformers, lines, and other equipment; two lines into Arco blew out before they found the right combination.

In the end, when Ray Haroldsen did throw the switch, nothing seemed to happen. The town, now lit with nuclear-produced electricity, looked the same as it had a few minutes before. But that meant the experiment had been successful.

Haroldsen said he suspected few people actually knew the difference. "Some who were up late may have wondered if something was going on," he said later, "as there were some company television people around."

He recalled that the day after, "Some international visitors toured the BORAX site and found the reactor and power plant in casual operation as if those tests had been routine."

Arco long hoped for an economic boom from the development at the federal facility, now called the Idaho National Engineering and Environmental Laboratory. That economic boost never occurred; most of the people and many of the facilities wound up being located in Idaho Falls, which did grow because of the federal activity. Arco today is much like it was back in 1955: a small crossroads town not far from the Craters of the Moon National Monument, a farm and cattle town. These days, Arco is back to getting its electric power from private, nonnuclear utilities.

But even today, Arco's city hall bears a sign proclaiming it the first city in the world to be lit by nuclear energy.

The Crash That Changed Idaho Politics

· 1966 ·

Charles Herndon, a Salmon attorney and the Democratic nominee for governor in a close, hotly contested race, was a man in a tight spot. On the morning of September 14, 1966, he had a serious logistical problem. Attempting to solve it would cost him his life.

That morning, cold and alternately drizzly and foggy, he was in Pocatello in southeast Idaho, where he had arrived on a campaign stop the night before. His schedule called for him to be at an event in Coeur d'Alene, in Idaho's Panhandle, at three o'clock that afternoon. It was much too far to drive in that amount of time—a trip of twelve hours or more.

Idaho, with its many high and rugged mountains rising up throughout its middle sections, never has been easy to navigate. Getting from eastern to northern Idaho on the ground, as a practical matter, always has meant heading all the way west to Boise, near the Oregon border, and then heading north; or else heading north deep into Montana, and then west through and over several ranges of mountains.

Herndon would have to fly.

And therein was the problem. Most of the airports in the area were closed down, fogged in. There were no regularly scheduled flights in southern Idaho that would arrive in Coeur d'Alene in time. Herndon drove to Twin Falls, where the weather was better, though still not good, and chartered a small plane to take him to Coeur d'Alene.

Herndon was in a tough race—tough because it could go either way. That year, 1966, had turned into an odd and unpredictable political year. His opponent was Don Samuelson, who had just defeated three-term Republican governor Robert Smylie in the primary. Samuelson was a hard-working candidate, but Democrats figured that in the general election he might be beaten and thought Herndon would be politically centrist enough to have a good chance at winning. Herndon had just won his own difficult primary, narrowly beating a young state senator named Cecil Andrus. Herndon's chances were good, but Herndon felt he could leave nothing to chance and was campaigning actively.

The stormy weather kept up as Herndon's small plane took off and headed north. The pilot ran into trouble around the high and jagged Sawtooth Mountains. Beset by rain and clouds, the plane smashed into Elk Mountain, in the center of the state.

It was the second plane crash that year involving a candidate for high office in Idaho. Earlier in the year, Republican congressional candidate John Mattmiller, flying his own plane, had crashed near his home in the Silver Valley. His replacement nominee for the seat turned out to be James McClure, who went on to win the House seat and spent twenty-four years in Congress, most of them in the Senate.

The Herndon crash launched another prominent Idaho political career. Orofino businessman Cecil Andrus, defeated in the primary, seemed to be moving away from politics when the crash occurred. Then his supporters urged him to seek the Democratic nomination for governor, and he did. At a contentious party convention, he narrowly defeated a candidate backed by Herndon's supporters. In the general election, he narrowly lost to Samuelson, but returned to defeat him in 1970, winning the first of his four terms as governor. Andrus went on to serve as secretary of the interior in President Jimmy Carter's cabinet.

Two plane crashes in a strange political year launched the illustrious careers of leading politicians of the late twentieth century in Idaho.

Jumping the Snake
· 1974 ·

O n Saturday, September 7, 1974, Tom Rauckhorst of Akron, Ohio, got on his motorcycle and tried to jump across the Snake River canyon near Twin Falls, Idaho. He failed.

Witnesses said he rode his motorcycle off the rim of the canyon, stayed in the air for about 150 feet, and then fell straight down into the Snake River. Rescued by people who had watched his attempt, he was taken to Magic Valley Memorial Hospital with compression fractures of the vertebrae, apparently caused when he hit the water.

Why did he do it? Well, famous daredevil Evel Knievel was going to try this stunt the next day.

Twin Falls is a relatively small farm and food-processing town, not a place where high-profile events happen very often. In the early days of September 1974, there were no motel rooms available in or near Twin Falls. People had come from all over the United States and Canada to witness "The Jump" and participate in the scene. Many were motorcyclists; some came in their recreational vehicles. Many came expecting a big party. The event even drew celebrities: Jack Ford, the son of President Gerald Ford, came to the canyon rim to see the action.

Tickets for access to the jump site were sold for $25 each, and about ten thousand people purchased them. Early publicity—and the publicity machine worked furiously on this event—had suggested fifty thousand might be there. At least as many watched from other vantage points—across the river or on buttes farther away. On the Saturday night before the jump, thousands of people rolled into the area to camp in unconventional places, waiting for the big event the next day.

Casual visitors, including almost everyone entering or leaving Twin Falls via the grand I. B. Perrine Bridge, could see the canyon easily enough. It is a dramatic thing: a flat desert plain split by a cut in the earth with sides that go almost straight down to the Snake River, which has been carving the canyon for millions of years. The distance from the south canyon rim to the north varies, but near Shoshone Falls east of Twin Falls, where Knievel planned to jump, it is about a third of a mile across, though Knievel planned to jump considerably farther to achieve a safe touchdown on the far side. The drop from the canyon rim into the river is about 500 feet.

To negotiate the crossing, Knievel had developed a special motorcycle—a skycycle—with rocket power. Knievel had been well known for years for jumping over barrels and cars on conventional motorcycles, but this was something different. He planned to use 5,000 pounds of thrust to power the machine up a 108-foot ramp, throwing him 3,000 feet in the air and keeping just enough forward momentum to put him down safely on the other side. At the right moment a special parachute would open and slow the vehicle just enough to reduce altitude and speed.

It didn't quite work out that way.

Knievel fired his rockets at 3:44 on Sunday afternoon, just a few minutes later than expected. His journey started well: He shot off the ramp exactly as predicted, and up, 500, then 1,000 feet into the air, midway over the canyon. It looked as if he would make it.

But the parachute came open too early; the cover on top of it blown off by the intense pressure almost at the moment Knievel took off. The fierce wind over the canyon caught it, ripped it open, and in seconds the skycycle, with Knievel inside, was off course.

Knievel's wife, Linda, and their three children were there to watch the event. As the skycycle vanished down into the canyon, she was heard to say, "Oh, my God."

Fortunately, slowed by the chute, the cycle fell straight into the canyon. The wind pulled it backward, toward the south canyon rim. About 70 feet above the river, the cycle smacked into the lava rock on the rim, bounced off, and landed on dry ground about 20 feet from the river's edge. Knievel later said that if his cycle had landed in the river instead of on the ground, he might have drowned because he was so thoroughly strapped in. Watchers were concerned that he might try to escape the cycle as it was falling; but that move, too, might have been fatal.

A rescue team watching the event in a nearby helicopter raced to the site, reaching the skycycle barely a minute after it hit the ground. They found that the daredevil had been lucky: Apart from a few small cuts and bruises, Evel Knievel was unharmed. Oddly, a member of the rescue crew received a more serious injury when the skycycle slid off the rock where it had come to rest and rolled down into the water.

The next day, Bob Truax, who had designed the skycycle, said he had torn up the check Knievel had given him for it. But at his evening press conference after the jump, Knievel said, "There was no Truax failure, there was no team failure, there was no Knievel failure."

He made it sound as if he might try the jump again: "Let's find the problem and do it again."

In the years since, there's been speculation from time to time about whether Knievel, his son Robbie, or someone else will take another run at traversing the canyon. As of yet, it has remained no more than talk.

The Teton Dam Flood
·1976·

Robbie Robison, the Bureau of Reclamation's point man at the agency's new Teton Dam, was concerned. The structural integrity of the dam had been in question for some time, but what was concerning Robison right now was the hot, late spring–early summer of May and June 1976, after much winter snow the season before. The snowpack was melting fast, and water was rising behind the dam much faster than he would have liked. In early June small leaks were spotted in the dam.

The dam, long sought by area farmers and strongly supported by Idaho's leading politicians, had been finished less than a year before. It backed up water on the Teton River, which started near the Teton Mountains on the Wyoming border and poured southeast into the Snake River, just north of Idaho Falls in the eastern part of the state.

Robison was still watching the dam closely on the morning of June 5, when he spotted a small leak, and then another. By the time they could investigate, workers found another big crack, and in midmorning Robison called the sheriffs of Fremont and Madison Counties—the dam and the Teton River itself straddled their borders—and urged them to evacuate residents.

Martha Black, who lived just a few miles downstream from the dam at Wilford, recalled: "It was that beautiful kind of June morning that is just right for working in the garden and yard. Warren, my husband, and I had just finished putting the final touches to our work and sat down in the lawn chairs admiring what we had accomplished. It was about 12:15, and we were almost ready to eat lunch when I heard someone pounding on our front door. It was so loud and hard that I ran to open it, to find a man with a serious, stern, red face and bulging eyes. He commanded me in a loud voice, 'Get out! Get out! Get out of your house! The Teton Dam has burst. The flood is coming!'"

Warren and Martha Black each grabbed a handful of personal belongings and raced to their cars. And, she recalled: "I gave one last look around our beautiful home, garden, yard, new garage, and hay crop, knowing that when we came back it would not be the same. I could hardly see to drive."

About two hours later, a family of tourists drove to the top of the canyon where the dam was located and turned on their movie camera. They recorded a spectacular scene: One side of the dam caved, the top of the dam fell into the reservoir, and the water gushed out, headed toward farms, homes, cities— and people.

It was, the book *Cadillac Desert* noted, "the second-largest flood in North America since the last Ice Age."

Brown water roared out of the valley and onto the flat Snake River plain. It looked from a distance like a huge dust storm, a cloud several stories high above the desert floor. But the water was enormously powerful. It smashed into the tiny community of Wilford and destroyed it completely, even ripping soil off the rocks, leaving not a chance of farming there again. Twenty-foot-high walls of water hit Sugar City, erasing most of the town. One house lifted up by the water, was tangled in an electric line and then exploded, the propane gas in the house having been ignited.

Now six feet high, the water poured into Rexburg, where most of the people had sought refuge on the hillside where Ricks College (now Brigham Young University–Idaho) was located. It continued down to Idaho Falls and finally came to rest about 100 miles from the Teton Dam, in the American Falls Reservoir.

Evacuation efforts had been successful. Neighbor passed the word to neighbor, and nearly everyone got out in time. Still, eleven people died, many more were injured, and property losses ran into the hundreds of millions of dollars.

Mrs. Black returned to Wilford on Sunday afternoon. "I thought I was prepared for what had happened. I was not! I could not even tell where houses had been. I was so disoriented I couldn't tell where I was until I saw part of our house that was still standing—one of the very few. Out of 150 homes in Wilford, 133 were gone."

Repairs and renovation took several years. Most people in the flooded area were members of the Church of Jesus Christ of Latter-day Saints, and the church undertook an aggressive effort to get the people of the area back on their feet. Federal and state assistance was quick and large scale as well. Many of the communities in the area, including Sugar City and Rexburg, have been thoroughly restored, and the most unusual thing about them is the large number of new buildings—built since 1976.

Over the years, talk has occasionally surfaced of rebuilding the Teton Dam, though no serious efforts have been made in that direction.

The flood has not been forgotten. Rexburg has a Teton Dam Flood museum. And just off Highway 33, east of the town of Newdale, visitors can still drive to the canyon overlooking the Teton River and see the remains of what was, briefly, the long-sought Teton Dam.

The Coming of Wilderness

· 1980 ·

Earl Dodds was stumped by the washing machine. It seemed to be the biggest intractable problem standing in the way of wilderness. With the conversion of the area he oversaw from "Primitive Area" to "Wilderness," a lot of modifications were happening in the way people lived in the deep backcountry. Dodds had been a ranger there for more than twenty years before the area was designated as wilderness, but once the orders came he took on the challenge aggressively.

There would be many changes as the Idaho Primitive Area became a wilderness. Many types of activities would have to stop, including the use of any kind of electrical or internal combustion engines in the area. Cars and trucks would be forbidden. The closest thing to an allowable exception was that planes still were to be allowed to land on some of the landing strips.

Dodds, the ranger in charge of a vast amount of land on the west side of the new Frank Church–River of No Return Wilderness, set to work on the changes. Some of them were easy. The workers quit using power saws and started using hand saws. "We learned to get the old cross cuts out and cut our fire wood," Dodds said. "It was quite a transformation."

The ranger station was not, never had been, connected to an electric grid, but like many occupied buildings in the backcountry, it did have an electric power generator that ran on gasoline. The Forest Service workers got rid of the generator and converted to propane lights.

"One thing had us stymied, and that was the washing machine," he said. "It was just too much to try to get people to do the laundry by hand and still be presentable." They were able to find a washing machine that ran on gasoline, but that still wasn't good enough. That machine still relied on a kind of internal combustion engine, and the National Forest Service employees had, as one of them said, "gotten the wilderness religion." They wanted to avoid any kind of machine that was not based on a natural process.

Finally they managed to solve even that problem. One of the NFS workers heard about a brilliant mechanic who lived in the tiny river community of Banks, west of the wilderness. They hauled the washing machine out to him, and he redesigned it to run on water power.

The next time NFS folks came by for a visit, Dodds eagerly showed off the washing machine as one of their most hard-won achievements.

The Wilderness Act of 1964 said that a wilderness is "at least five thousand acres of land or is of sufficient size as to make practicable its preservation and use in an unimpaired condition." Nationally, about 105 million acres of land are included in the wilderness system. The Frank Church–River of No Return Wilderness is one of the largest, at about 2.3 million acres.

Idaho now has seven wilderness areas. In recent years most of them have become major tourist attractions; outfitters and guides routinely take an increasing number of visitors through them.

The Poacher
· 1981 ·

Jim Stevens was only visiting Claude Dallas, the trapper, just delivering mail and camping supplies, on January 5. They were in the remote Owyhee Mountains country, far from any city or town, and Dallas did not often get visitors out here other than Stevens. But on this day, as Stevens walked back to the camp after a quick search for Indian arrowheads near a dry river bottom, he was surprised to see that Dallas was not alone.

His visitors were Idaho Fish and Game officers, Bill Pogue and Conley Elms. A nearby rancher, who suspected Dallas was poaching—hunting out of season and using illegally baited traps—had tipped them off to Dallas's activities. Stories about Dallas's poaching activities were common in the area, and Pogue, a senior conservation officer who had been a police chief in Nevada, knew with whom he was dealing.

Dallas had learned poaching during his days growing up in Michigan and Ohio, and after coming west to work on cattle ranches, he kept at it. This season he was especially keen on bobcats; their fur would fetch as much as $285 per animal. Dallas caught more than many trappers did because he fussed much less than most with the legal requirements. Poaching in some of the remotest country on the continent over the years, he had managed to avoid getting caught.

Now his luck had run out. On this day, the evidence—the illegally taken bobcats, the shot deer, the raccoon pelt, and much more—was all around them, some of it in plain view and some in Dallas's tent. Dallas was offering excuses, but Pogue wasn't buying them.

The usually strong canyon wind had stopped. The tension in the still air, in the serene quiet, was almost overwhelming.

Stevens asked, "How far are we into Idaho?"—meaning, how far north of the Nevada state line.

"About 3 miles," Pogue replied.

Dallas countered, "I guess you know I'm going to tell the judge I got those hides in Nevada."

The officers continued to look at the furs, and Dallas finally said, "Are you going to take me in?"

Dallas would later maintain—though Stevens said he never heard it—that Pogue replied, "You can go easy or you can go hard." Dallas said he took that to mean Pogue might kill him.

But seconds later, Dallas did the killing. Making moves he had practiced after years of reading western novels and watching western movies, he swiftly pulled out his hidden pistol, crouched into firing position, and shot Pogue—who called out, "Oh, no!" as the bullet hit him in the chest—and then Elms. A minute later, Dallas walked over to where they lay on the ground and shot each man in the head.

Stevens, completely stunned, moaned, "Why Claude, why?"

He said later that Dallas had sworn he would never be arrested again. He had been, years before, for draft evasion.

Dallas hid the bodies and made a trip back south into Nevada, where he went to the home of a close friend in Paradise Valley, north of Winnemucca. Stevens went home to his wife in that city. After talking with her, he decided to call the police. The hunt for Claude Dallas, which would last for more than a year, until the spring of 1981, quickly got underway. During that time, Dallas traveled across much of North America, but finally he returned to Nevada, and there in the desert he was finally trapped himself, by police SWAT teams.

Tried and convicted of voluntary manslaughter in a trial that made headlines across the West, Dallas was sentenced to three 10-year prison terms. But in March 1986, using bolt cutters to slice through the Idaho prison fence, he escaped. Another manhunt, this one lasting eight months, ensued, until Dallas finally was caught again outside a convenience store in Riverside, California. (Astonishingly, he was acquitted by an Idaho jury of the crime of escape.) He has been in prison ever since, most recently in a Kansas penitentiary. He is scheduled for release in 2005.

Dallas has defenders, people who dislike government and see the trapper as one of the last vestiges of an older era of the West. To others, probably to most, he is simply a killer.

The Last Stoplight
· 1990 ·

The plan called for demolishing most of downtown Wallace
so that Interstate 90 could be run through it.

The Federal Highway Administration didn't have many
options. In this particular part of northern Idaho, the mountains
were constant, and there was one valley through them. In some
places the valley widened but here, at Wallace, the mountains
rose up sharply on either side of town, north and south. Even
many houses were built on steep hillsides.

For decades drivers coming from the west rode an interstate highway to the edge of town, then slowed to a crawl on
a suddenly narrow, bumpy road that snaked through downtown Wallace. Usually, they'd have to halt for a stoplight at
Bank Street, about a block from the county courthouse. A mile
later, leaving town, the interstate started again.

It was the last stoplight on the road from Seattle to Boston.

Finally the federal highway officials decided the time had
come to push on through. They made plans to build the road
through the center of Wallace, leveling much of the old, historic
mining city.

They failed to reckon with Harry Magnuson. Magnuson
was an accountant by trade who had become wealthy invest-
ing in local mining companies during their glory years. He had
become a businessman with far-flung interests; but he chose to
keep living in little Wallace. He simply loved the unusual, historic town. Many of its buildings and businesses, especially
those downtown, dated back to the region's raucous mining

days, though the heydays of mining were a thing of the past. No other community in Idaho had anything similar.

Now, determined to stop the federal government from destroying Wallace's heritage, he drove an hour west to the Coeur d'Alene law office of Scott Reed.

Reed, one of the top attorneys in northern Idaho, liked to take on cases protecting the environment, and he and Magnuson often had squared off over the interests of the local mining companies. But on this day he walked into Reed's office and said, "Scott, you gotta help me out."

Scott did. Magnuson said, "We'll file suit against the highway department, the federal government, and everybody in the world." With their initial lawsuit, filed in 1970, they stopped construction activity cold after a federal district judge in Boise agreed with them that the historic area should not be demolished. For the better part of two decades, the two sides tussled, as the last stoplight on I–90 continued to give drivers pause.

Finally, after many years, the two sides reached a compromise. The city agreed to being bypassed by the freeway. Up to this point, it had reaped some benefits by being a place where travelers simply had to slow down.

On the other hand, Magnuson said that the federal planners and others involved with highway construction "have become much more conscious of the aesthetic, economic, and people impact."

The highway planners came up with a way to build the interstate nearby on the north hillside on what amounted to a high bridge over the town. The historic parts of Wallace, including the whole of the downtown area, remained intact.

Today, many travelers zip past the city of Wallace through the narrow, winding canyon on the stretch of the interstate that overlooks the town.

But some, a little more knowledgeable about the background of the area, still take the east exit, wind through town on the business loop, and pause at the stoplight on Bank Street.

To the Moon in Idaho

· 1999 ·

It was a revisitation, a recollection of earlier days, and a revival of hope. The place was Idaho's bleakest desert, a flat, hot, desolate place. Even the nearby habitable area called the Lost River Valley had a modest population.

The visitors were Edgar Mitchell, Joe Engle, and Eugene Cernan. Though their names were no longer household words in most of America, they were beloved celebrities at the desert town of Arco, where they were meeting and greeting, attending receptions, and speaking to student groups.

They had history in common. Three decades before, when they were pioneering astronauts, they had trained here—right after Neil Armstrong and Buzz Aldrin had become the first men to set foot on the moon.

Their training program had been long and rigorous, and it covered a great deal. What conventional training barely touched, however, was one thing important for these astronauts who soon would visit the moon to know: geology. The program they were part of, the Apollo lunar program, was planned to bring back to Earth samples of the moon—it eventually would bring back 243 pounds of lunar rocks—so the astronauts had to be taught what samples to get. Besides that, some extra training for walking on the harsh, jagged lunar surface, so pockmarked with astral debris that it little resembles the surface of Earth, would help too.

So on August 22, 1969, about a month after the first walk on the moon, Mitchell, Engle, Cernan, and Alan Shepherd were flown on an Air Force C-54 first to Idaho's Mountain Home Air Force Base, then to Arco. Receiving a handful of gifts from Idahoans, Shepherd said some souvenir might make it to the moon with him but quipped, "I don't think even Idaho potatoes would grow on the moon by what I've heard." Then the astronauts drove into the desert to the Craters of the Moon National Monument.

Craters was designated as a national monument back in 1924, its weird, dangerous landscape impossible either to ignore or underestimate. It is a massive lava flow, one of the most recent in North America, located over a still-unstable geologic rip called the Great Rift. The flows are cold, black, and solid but still so recent that erosion has barely touched them. The area has an austere beauty, but it is resistant to life and dangerous to the unwary. Nature has been uncommonly resourceful here; the region is home to many plants and animals. However, much of the Craters region is simply uninhabitable and impassable for people, though a few protected walking trails have been developed near the monument's visitor's center.

The astronauts put in what they called "a good day's work" hiking on and around the lava flows and studying the geology of the area. The geologic forms, they said, were ideal learning tools for those about to head for the moon. Later in the day they flew to Idaho Falls to learn more about geology at a pumice pit near the town of Ammon.

Three months shy of thirty years later, Mitchell, Cernan, and Engle (Shepherd had died in 1998) returned to Craters to celebrate the seventy-fifth anniversary of the monument and the thirtieth anniversary of the first lunar landing.

They spoke to groups large and small around Arco and Idaho Falls. On their third day in the area, a Saturday, they visited Craters once again, walking back over the same lava flows. They noted that in many ways, at Craters and at Arco, a great deal they remembered from their visit of so many years before had remained unchanged.

Throughout their visit, looking back and looking ahead, they had a consistent message. Cernan put it most succinctly: "Dream, dream, dream, then follow through with commitment and make it happen."

A Potpourri of Idaho Facts

- Idaho is the thirteenth largest state, encompassing 83,557 square miles, only 800 of which are covered with water.

- Some Idaho references say, and many Idahoans believe, that the state's name is an Indian word for "gem of the mountains." However appealing, the story isn't true. The word was probably coined by western prospectors in the 1850s; Colorado, which had a gold rush shortly before the first of Idaho's gold rushes, nearly was called "Idaho."

- Idaho's unusual shape has led to some unusual border lengths. The border with British Columbia, Canada, on the north, is only about 40 miles wide. But on the south, Idaho's borders with Nevada and Utah run an estimated 305 miles. The state is 470 miles from north to south.

- The official state song is "Here We Have Idaho." The song, originally known as "Garden of Paradise," was composed over a period of years by three writers working separately.

- Idaho's state seal is the only one designed by a woman. The drawing, highlighting the state's mining, forestry, and agriculture industries, was designed by Emma Sarah Etine Edwards, and was chosen in a contest in 1891.

- The largest stand of the western white pine trees in the United States grows in northern Idaho. The western white pine was designated the state's official tree in 1935.

- Idaho has 44 counties, 201 cities, and 113 school districts.

- Seven of Idaho's counties—Butte, Camas, Clark, Custer, Idaho, Lemhi, Owyhee—are home to fewer than two persons per square mile.

- The largest city in Idaho is the capital, Boise. The smallest is Warm River, which never has reported a population of more than a dozen people.

- Downtown Boise is rich with geothermal water resources. All of the Capitol Mall buildings are heated with geothermal water, as are many of the houses along one of the city's premier drives, Warm Springs Boulevard.

- Federal agencies, primarily the U.S. Forest Service and Bureau of Land Management, manage 63.7 percent of all land in Idaho. Thirty-one percent of the state's land is in private hands.

- Idaho was regularly ranked in the 1990s and in the 2000 census as one of the fastest-growing states in the country. The large counties of Ada, Canyon, and Kootenai account for almost all of the increase in population, while some small counties have lost population.

- Idaho often is said to have three capitals—in an economic and cultural, if not political, sense—Boise in the southwest; Salt Lake City, Utah, in the southeast; and Spokane, Washington, in the north.

- Soda Springs has the largest captive geyser in the world and is also home to natural springs. The area was a popular stop for Oregon and California Trail travelers.

- The notorious Wyatt Earp spent time in and around Eagle City.

- Geographically, the state is almost exactly halfway between the North Pole and the equator. A sign marking the location of 45 degrees latitude is located on Highway 55 just north of New Meadows, not far from the halfway mark between Idaho's northern and southern boundaries.

- Idaho has just two metropolitan areas: Boise, which includes Ada and Canyon Counties, and Pocatello, which includes Bannock County. For many years Pocatello was the second-largest city in the state, but the 2000 census revealed that Nampa, located near Boise, had grown so fast, it had become the second largest.

- The Salmon River, which arises in the Sawtooth Mountains near Stanley and pours into the Snake River west of Grangeville, is the longest river in the United States that is contained entirely in one state. It is called the "River of No Return" because it is difficult to navigate against its swift currents and rapids.

- Idaho has two major sand dune areas. The Bruneau Dunes near the town of Bruneau have been designated as a state park. In eastern Idaho, near St. Anthony, vacationers visit the larger St. Anthony Sand Dunes, which are 35 miles long and 5 miles wide.

- Idaho is the only state divided on an east–west line between time zones. Northern Idaho, in general north of the Salmon

River, is in the Pacific time zone, and southern Idaho is in the Mountain time zone.

- The highest spot in Idaho is the peak of Mount Borah in Custer County, at 12,662 feet above sea level. The lowest spot is at Lewiston, 770 feet above sea level.

- Although located far inland, Idaho has one seaport, at Lewiston. Farm and other products are barged from there down the Snake River to the Columbia River, and ultimately, to the Pacific Ocean.

- There are five Indian reservations in Idaho. The Shoshone-Bannock (Fort Hall) reservation is located in eastern Idaho and the Nez Percé, Coeur d'Alene, and Kootenai reservations are located in northern Idaho. The Shoshone-Paiute reservation, called Duck Valley, straddles the border between Idaho and Nevada; most of its people live in Nevada.

- Idaho has one of the largest Basque communities in the United States, and a major Basque cultural center is located in downtown Boise.

- Idaho ranks first in the nation for production of three plant crops: potatoes, Austrian winter peas, and wrinkled seed peas. It also ranks first in the nation for production of hatchery trout, an industry concentrated in the Hagerman and Buhl area.

- Two Idaho politicians, both nationally known United States senators, have run for president. They were Republican William Borah in 1936 and Democrat Frank Church in 1976. Idaho Senator Glen Taylor ran for vice president on the Progressive Party ticket in 1948.

- Through Idaho's history, more people have come to the state from, and have left the state for, California than any other state.

- Idaho's two largest private employers are both high-technology companies. Micron Technology in Boise is a major producer of computer microchips, and Bechtel BWXT Idaho of Idaho Falls is the prime contractor at the Idaho National Engineering and Environmental Laboratory.

- Actress Lana Turner was born in Burke, Idaho. Poet Ezra Pound, baseball player Harmon Killebrew, and champion skier Picabo Street are also from Idaho.

- During World War II, a Japanese internment camp was located in south central Idaho, near Jerome.

- Idaho has state universities at Moscow (University of Idaho), Boise (Boise State University), and Pocatello (Idaho State University).

- Although much of Idaho is relatively temperate, the state does see some weather extremes. The highest temperature on record is 118 degrees at Orofino on July 28, 1934. The lowest is -60 degrees at Island Park Dam on January 18, 1943.

- Idaho has seven federally designated wilderness areas. Two of them, the Selway-Bitterroot and the Frank Church-River of No Return, each contain more than a million acres.

- The Hagerman Fossil Bed National Monument near Hagerman is one of the four largest fossil deposits found anywhere in North America. The Hagerman Horse, which was discovered there and ranged in the southern part of the state more than three million years ago, has been designated as Idaho's state fossil.

- Several thousand square miles in eastern Idaho, often called "Hell's Half-Acre," is covered by lava rock only a few thousand years old. Though no longer hot, some of it still is so sharp that ordinary shoes can be sliced to pieces from walks on it. The vast spread of this rock accounts for a huge expanse of eastern Idaho in which no human settlement (and only limited animal settlement) ever has occurred. This area has been put to use, however; it was used to train astronauts headed to the moon.

- Idaho is a place of geologic ferment. More than two dozen volcanic eruptions and more than sixty lava flows have shaped large parts of the state.

- Hells Canyon on the Oregon border generally is considered to be the deepest canyon in the United States.

Bibliography

Andrus, Cecil, and Joel Connelly. *Politics Western Style*. Seattle, WA: Sasquatch Books, 1998.

Ashby, LeRoy, and Rod Gramer. *Against the Odds: The Life of Senator Frank Church*. Pullman, WA: Washington State University Press, 1994.

Batt, Phil. *The Compleat Phil Batt*. Boise: self-published, printed by Caxton Printers, 1999.

Bunderson, Harold R. *Idaho Entrepreneurs*. Boise, ID: Boise State University Press, 1992.

Carrey, John, Cort Conley, and Ace Barton. *Snake River of Hells Canyon*. Cambridge, ID: Backeddy Books, 1979.

Colson, Dennis C. *Idaho's Constitution: The Tie That Binds*. Moscow: University of Idaho Press, 1991.

Conley, Cort. *Idaho for the Curious*. Cambridge, ID: Backeddy Books, 1982.

———. *Idaho Loners: Hermits, Solitaries and Individualists*. Cambridge, ID: Backeddy Books, 1994.

Drury, Clifford. *Henry Harmon Spalding*. Caldwell, ID: Caxton Printers, 1936.

Elsensohn, Sister Mary Alfreda. *Polly Bemis*. Cottonwood, ID: Idaho Corporation of Benedictine Sisters, 1979.

Fazio, James R. *Across the Snowy Ranges: The Lewis and Clark Expedition in Idaho and Western Montana*. Moscow, ID: Woodland Press, 2001.

Fisher, Vardis, ed. *Idaho: A Guide in Word and Picture*. Caldwell, ID: Caxton Printers, 1937.

Gowans, Fred. *Rocky Mountain Rendezvous*. Provo, UT: Brigham Young University, 1976.

Greene, Jerome A. *Nez Percé Summer 1877*. Helena, MT: Montana Historical Society Press, 2000.

Grover, David H. *Diamondfield Jack: A Study in Frontier Justice*. Reno: University of Nevada Press, 1968.

Hunt, Ruby. *Northwest Disaster: Avalanche and Fire*. Portland, OR: Binford & Mort, 1960.

Idaho Blue Book. Published periodically in odd-numbered years by the Office of the Idaho Secretary of State.

Idaho Yesterdays. Boise: Idaho Historical Society, published quarterly.

Johnson, Claudius O. *Borah of Idaho*. New York: Longmans, Green & Co., 1936.

Josephy, Alvin M., Jr. *The Nez Percé Indians and the Opening of the Northwest*. New Haven, CT: Yale University Press, 1965.

Lavender, David. *Let Me Be Free: The Nez Percé Tragedy*. New York: HarperCollins, 1992.

Limbaugh, Ronald H. *Rocky Mountain Carpetbaggers: Idaho's Territorial Governors*. Moscow: University Press of Idaho, 1982.

Lukas, J. Anthony. *Big Trouble*. New York: Simon & Schuster, 1997.

Madsen, Brigham. *The Bannock of Idaho*. Caldwell, ID: Caxton Printers, 1958.

The Official Idaho Travel Guide. Boise: Idaho Department of Commerce, revised annually.

Olsen, Jack. *Give a Boy a Gun: A True Story of Law and Disorder in the American West*. New York: Delacorte Press, 1985.

Oppenheimer, Doug, and Jim Poore. *Sun Valley: A Biography*. Boise. ID: Beatty Books, 1976.

Palmer, Tim. *The Snake River*. Washington, DC: Island Press, 1991.

Pearce, Neal. *The Rocky Mountain States of America*. New York: W. W. Norton & Co., 1972.

Peterson, F. Ross. *Idaho*. New York: W. W. Norton & Co., 1976.

Plastino, Ben. *Coming of Age: Idaho Falls and the Idaho National Engineering Laboratory*. Boise: published posthumously by family, 1998.

Reisner, Marc. *Cadillac Desert*. New York: Penguin Books, 1986.

Schwantes, Carlos A. *In Mountain Shadows: A History of Idaho*. Lincoln: University of Nebraska Press, 1991.

Shallatt, Todd, ed. *The Snake: The Plain and Its People*. Boise, ID: Boise State University Press, 1995.

Sims, Robert, ed. *The Governors of Idaho*. Boise, ID: Boise State University, 1991.

Smylie, Robert, ed. *Governor Smylie Remembers*. Moscow: University of Idaho Press, 1998.

Stacy, Susan, ed. *Conversations*. Boise: Idaho Public Television Broadcasting Foundation, 1990.

Stapilus, Randy. *Paradox Politics: People and Power in Idaho.* Boise, ID: Ridenbaugh Press, 1988.

Swisher, Perry. *The Day Before Idaho.* Moscow, ID: News Review Publishing, 1995.

Taylor, Glen. *The Way It Was With Me.* New York: Lyle Stuart, 1979.

———. *That Day In June.* Rexburg, ID: Ricks College Press, 1977.

Walker, Deward. *Indians of Idaho.* Moscow: University Press of Idaho, 1982.

Wells, Merle. *Anti-Mormonism in Idaho, 1872–92.* Provo, UT: Brigham Young University Press, 1978.

Woodward, Tim. *Tiger on the Road: The Life of Vardis Fisher.* Caldwell, ID: Caxton Printers, 1989.

Index

About the Author

As a newspaper columnist, reporter, and author of a book about Idaho's political history, *Paradox Politics,* Randy Stapilus has written about Idaho for more than a quarter of a century. He edits four newsletters on northwest public affairs and natural resources. Mr. Stapilus has lived in all the corners of Idaho, and currently lives in Boise.